The Story of Be

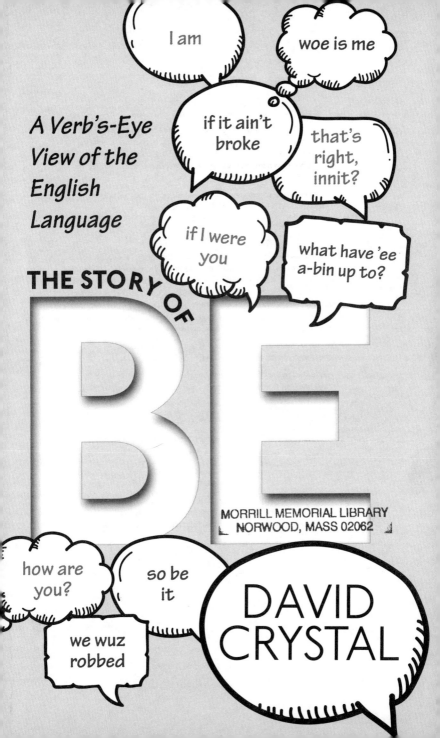

420
Crystal

OXFORD
UNIVERSITY PRESS

Great Clarendon Street, Oxford, OX2 6DP,
United Kingdom

Oxford University Press is a department of the University of Oxford.
It furthers the University's objective of excellence in research, scholarship,
and education by publishing worldwide. Oxford is a registered trade mark of
Oxford University Press in the UK and in certain other countries

© David Crystal 2017
© the cartoon illustrations on pp. xiii, 16, 42, 64, 106, 114, 148, 170
Ed McLachlan 2017

The moral rights of the author have been asserted

Impression: 1

Published in the United States of America by Oxford University Press
198 Madison Avenue, New York, NY 10016, United States of America

British Library Cataloguing in Publication Data

Data available

Library of Congress Control Number: 2016948369

ISBN 978-0-19-879109-6

Printed in Great Britain by
Clays Ltd, St Ives plc

CONTENTS

Contents

PANELS

PREFACE

Lexicographers like to tell the story of a reader who brings a dictionary back to a lending library and comments to the librarian: 'Quite enjoyable, but the stories are rather short, aren't they.' Well, it would have depended on which dictionary the reader had borrowed. It wouldn't be possible to say that about the unabridged *Oxford English Dictionary*.

The reader was right about one thing: a dictionary *is* a collection of stories. Each word has a unique tale to tell, and nothing tells those tales better than a historical dictionary. There is, moreover, a bonus. A dictionary is a portal through which we gain access to the word-hoard of meanings and uses accumulated throughout the history of a language. Whichever word we choose, we find ourselves engaging with the story of the language as a whole. And if we choose *be*, we encounter a special insight into English, and into the society and thought that has shaped it over the past 1,500 years.

Thanks to its remarkable history, *be* has developed a greater range of meanings and uses, and a wider range of variant forms, than any other English word—1,812 so far recorded by the *OED* lexicographers, both in the standard language and in regional dialects. The uses of *be* described in this book reflect their findings, and correspond, for the most part, to the senses distinguished in the huge *be* entry in the dictionary. If we take its eight elements together—*be, am, are, is, was, were, being, been*—it turns out to be the second most frequent item in English, after *the*. So if our library reader is looking for a good story, it is likely to be found here.

Why are there so many forms? To answer that question, we need to go back into prehistory.

PROLOGUE

In the beginning…

…were three verbs.

Around 4,500 years ago, a people living in the steppes of western Asia spoke a language that has been called Indo-European, because it is the ancestor of many of the languages spoken in India and Europe in historical times. Detailed comparison of these languages has allowed philologists to reconstruct many features of this ancestral 'parent'. They found three distinct and unrelated verbs lying behind later manifestations of 'be', and all three appear in Modern English.

One verb had a set of forms that would eventually give rise to *am* and *is*, along with their dialect variants, and the forms *sie* and *sind* in Old English. At first sight, it seems unlikely that two such different words as *am* and *is* have a common origin; but you can get a hint of how they related to each other if you compare their two Sanskrit relatives below. *Are* and *art* may also belong with this set, though some scholars think they are so different that they must have had a separate origin.

- Related forms for *am* include *asmi* in Sanskrit, *jam* in Albanian, and *sum* in Latin.
- Related forms for *is* include *asti* in Sanskrit, *ist* in German, and *est* in Latin.
- Related forms for *sie* and *sind* include *santi* in Sanskrit, *sind* in German, and *sunt* in Latin.

The second verb would eventually give rise to Modern English *be*, *being*, and *been*, along with their dialect variants. This verb in Indo-European seems originally to have meant 'become, grow'.

+ Related forms include *fui* and *fieri* in Latin, *bin* in German, and *ben* in Dutch.

The third verb would eventually give rise to Modern English *was* and *were*, along with their dialect variants. This verb in Indo-European seems originally to have meant 'remain, stay'.

+ Related forms include *wesan* in Old High German and *vesa* in Old Icelandic.

It is this multiple history that gives *be* its unusual character—seen also in other languages, such as Latin, French, and German. Notions of 'being' must have formed an important element in the minds of the Indo-Europeans. The special status of *be* is shown in several ways:

+ It has more variant forms than any other English verb. Most verbs have just a single base that is used throughout: *walk*, *walks*, *walking*, *walked*. *Go* is another exception, with *go*, *goes*, *going*, *gone*, and *went*. But nothing matches the variants found in the history of *be*.
+ All English verbs mark just one person in the present tense, the 3rd person singular: *walks* versus (for all other persons) *walk*. But *be* has different forms for 1st, 2nd, and 3rd persons.
+ *Be* has both a stressed and an unstressed form: we see *be* and *been* alongside *bi* and *bin/bn*.
+ *Be* can occur with an attached pronoun in such forms as *twas* ('it was') and *wast* ('was it'). It also has contracted forms, as in

you're and *I'm*, and negative forms in which *n't* can be added (*aren't*, *weren't*). The only other main verbs that perform similarly are *have* and *do*—as in *hasn't* and *don't*.

+ *Be* has three very different grammatical functions. It can be used as a full verb, with such meanings as 'exist'. It can be used as an auxiliary verb to form more complex verb forms (as in *I am going*, *I was asked*). And it can be used as a way of linking the subject to the complement of a clause—the 'copular' function (as in *I am ready*, *Mary is a doctor*). No other English verb displays such functional diversity.

It is thus hardly surprising to find that, over the past 1,500 years, *be* has developed a wide range of meanings and uses, and a wider range of variant forms than any other English verb. It is the second most frequent word in English, after *the*. If any verb deserves its own story, it is this one.

1

To be or not to be

existential *be*

The bare *be*. Capable of being used as a single-word sentence—in grammatical terms, as an imperative. For those imagining a primordial act of creation, a word that brings everything into existence. For those offering counsel to others worried about the past or the future, a word that focuses on 'living in the now'. For those advising on contemporary fashion, a word that connotes a bold and confident self-image.

People are aware of the power that lies within this word and use it accordingly. It turns up in some unexpected places. Simply Be is a firm that deals in women's fashion. Be Unlimited is an internet service provider. 'Be', unmodified, is the name of several pop songs, such as those by Slade and Jessica Simpson. American rapper Common released his sixth album in 2005, and called it *Be*. The title track ends with a summarizing couplet:

Never looking back, or too far in front of me
The present is a gift, and I just want to be.

The title mystified some fans, who looked for hidden meanings; but in an interview for SixShot.com that year Common made it clear that there was nothing mysterious about it at all:

> I named it *Be* to be who you are, man, and be able to be in the moment and not try too hard.

'I just want to be', or 'wanna be', he might have said, thereby quoting several other songs with exactly that title.

It's a verb that evidently had a special attraction for P. G. Wodehouse's character Rockmetteller Todd in the story of 'The Aunt and the Sluggard' (1919), who writes poems like this:

> Be!
> Be!
> The past is dead.
> To-morrow is not born.
> Be to-day!
> To-day!
> Be with every nerve,
> With every muscle,
> With every drop of your red blood!
> Be!

Bertie Wooster explains:

> It was printed opposite the frontispiece of a magazine with a sort of scroll round it, and a picture in the middle of a fairly-nude chappie, with bulging muscles, giving the rising sun the glad eye. Rocky said they gave him a hundred dollars for it, and he stayed in bed till four in the afternoon for over a month.

Be, it seems, can make you money.

The opening definition in the *Oxford English Dictionary* (*OED*) adds an academic tone:

> I. Without required complement: to have or take place in the world of fact, to exist, occur, happen.

And then:

> To have place in the objective universe or realm of fact, to exist; (*spec.* of God, etc.) to exist independently of other beings. Also: to exist in life, to live. Now *literary*.

The biblical perspective is there from the very first citation: the 'I am who I am' of Exodus, Chapter 3—in Old English, 'Ic eom se þe eom' (for the pronunciation of Old English, see the Appendix). And similar usages permeate the many religious texts that have survived from the first thousand years of English, sometimes ringing the changes on the existential use of the verb with rhetorical ease:

> All things that are, or euer were, or shall hereafter bee.

That's from *A woorke concerning the trewnesse of the Christian religion*—a translation of a French text by Sir Philip Sidney and Arthur Golding in 1587. Some fifteen years later, Shakespeare gives us 'To be or not to be . . .'.

A citation from *The Independent* in 2004 reinforces the *OED*'s feeling that this sense of the verb remains 'literary' today:

> After 58 years the BBC's *Letter from America*, the world's longest-running speech radio programme, is no more.

It's the stylistic tone that allowed the Monty Python team to use it for great comedic effect in their famous dead-parrot sketch:

> This parrot is no more. It has ceased to be.

To *be no more*: an expression normally used when we want to add gravitas to a report of someone's death. And also an element of nostalgia: if we say that someone or something 'is no more', we convey that we are really feeling the loss. The point comes across most obviously in *OED* citations such as 'when youth and beauty are no more' and 'dreaming of days that are no more'. There's a hint of poetry in them.

The grammatical construction illustrated by my last sentence is usually called 'existential *there*'. I could have written: *A hint of poetry is in them*, but I wanted to give *a hint of poetry* extra emphasis, which it receives when it's placed after the verb. The *there* then fills the subject slot in the sentence, as required by English grammar.

This use of *there* has been in the language since Old English. Although related to *there* meaning a physical location, it's used in a very different way. When *there* refers to a location, it has a strong stress, and can occur later in a sentence, as in:

There's the book, on the table. [= The book is there, on the table.]

We can't do this with existential *there*, which is always unstressed, and is found only at the beginning of the sentence, as in:

There's a book on the table. [= A book is on the table.]

Here, I'm not pointing to the book's physical location, but rather bringing the book to my listener's attention—making whoever I'm talking to aware of its existence.

Other forms of *be* can be used in the same way:

There are apples on the tree.
There were lots of people there.
There's been another burglary.
There's a bottle of milk in the fridge.

4

And that last example points us towards the interesting case of *there's* acting as a fused unit, capable of being followed by a plural noun phrase even though the verb is singular:

There's bottles of milk in the fridge.

It's a usage that angers prescriptive grammarians, who expect agreement in number between the verb and the following noun phrase, and formal standard English avoids it; but it's very common in informal speech and writing, especially when the speaker is thinking of the noun phrase as if it referred to a single entity. Sometimes, indeed, the alternative form (*there are*) is impossible or hugely artificial:

There's lots of time before the train goes. [*never*: There are lots of time…]
There's some people been asking after you. [*never*: There are some people…]
Who's coming to the party? Well, there's John, Jim, and Tom for a start.

There's seems to act like an idiom, a fixed unit, in such cases. And that isn't the only idiomatic use of existential *be*. William Tyndale in his translation of the Bible gave us 'the powers that be' (Romans 13) to mean 'the authorities, those in control', and its future as an English idiom was assured when the expression was taken over without change by the translators of the King James Bible. Another is *let be*, meaning 'leave off, leave undisturbed'. This too has had a long life, both with and without an accompanying pronoun or noun phrase, as in these Shakespearean examples:

Soft you, let me be.   (*Much Ado about Nothing*)
Ah let be, let be, thou art / The armourer of my heart.   (*Antony and Cleopatra*)

5

But for present-day readers—at least, for those over a certain age—
the most famous instance of this use of existential *be* is much more
recent. From 1970, in fact, when the Beatles had a hit with the title
track of their final studio album: *Let It Be.*

The infinitive form: be

O NE of the oldest word-books in English is the *Corpus
Glossary*, compiled some time in the eighth century by
the monks at Canterbury to help them with their Latin. It has
been described as 'the oldest English dictionary'. In it, several
thousand Latin words, in alphabetical order, are given equivalents in Old English; and very early in the list we see *aporia-
mur*. It is translated as *biað þreade*—'are afflicted'. Is this the
earliest evidence of the verb *to be* in English?

That depends on how you date the Ruthwell Cross in
Dumfriesshire, south-west Scotland. There, in runes, are
some lines in Old English from a poem that we now know as
'The Dream of the Rood' (a poetic outpouring by the cross
on which Jesus Christ was crucified). One line reads: *Krist
wæs on rodi*—'Christ was on the cross'. Some have dated this
to the end of the seventh century.

Forms of *be* are scattered throughout the pieces gathered
together by Henry Sweet in the book he compiled in 1885 for
the Early English Text Society: *The Oldest English Texts.*
Along with some other grammatical words such as *in* and
on, they show the emerging grammatical character of the
language. There is considerable continuity between Old

English and Modern English, obscured by the largely alien vocabulary, and nothing represents this continuity more than the various forms of *be*.

The base form shown in Old English grammars is *beon*, 'to be', with the *e* sounded long, and in quality closer to present-day *bay* than *bee*. Some dialect variations are recorded, such as *bian*, *bion*, and *ben*, and there was also an inflected form, seen in *beonne* and *bene*, which seems to have died out by 1500. The *-n* forms continue into early Middle English, and stay on later in regional dialects, but the standard form without the *-n* is already emerging by the end of the thirteenth century. There's a huge amount of manuscript variation. Chaucer's *Franklin's Tale* has a line 'Love wol nat been constreyned by maistrye' ('love will not be constrained by mastery'): the various surviving manuscripts show *be*, *ben*, *bene*, *been*, and *buen*.

By 1600—the time of the most famous use of the infinitive in the history of English, Hamlet's *to be or not to be* soliloquy—the standard form was *be*, occasionally spelled *bee*. Regional variations continue, and are still seen in dialect writing today, usually reflecting local pronunciation, such as *bea* (Yorkshire), *beigh* (Derbyshire), *beo* (Northumberland), *ba* (Wexford), and *been* (southern USA), but sometimes graphically reinforcing a regional identity through a non-standard spelling, such as *bie* or *bee*. The unstressed form of *be* (as in *I must be going*), always pronounced with a short vowel, is sometimes written *bi*. In seventeenth-century poetry, we

7

see it also shown using an apostrophe, as in 'Thou must b'a King', 'To b'Englands Generall'.

Old English displays some unusual features. *Wesan*, the *be*-verb that would later give rise to *was* and *were* (Panels on p. 92 and p. 110), is occasionally used as an infinitive form, especially in Northumbria. 'Ic mæg wesan god swa he' ('I can be a god as well as he'), writes the scribe in the poem known as *Genesis B*. And *beon* could be used with a prefix: *ætbeon* meant 'to be present, to be at hand'; *frambeon* meant 'to be absent, to be away from'. We no longer coin verbs in this way, although *unbe* 'to be or make non-existent' has examples recorded into the nineteenth century, and doubtless still has nonce usages today. Apart from that, the adverb *maybe*, and the modern coinage *wannabe* (see Chapter 12), *be* remains unprefixed—and unsuffixed, apart from a single Shakespearean instance that was evidently so memorable that it remains an idiom today. Macbeth wishes that his murderous act 'Might be the be-all and the end-all'. This is one of the intriguing things about *be*: the way English speakers have kept its separate identity. It's almost as if they were proud of it.

"SUIT YOUR TALK TO YOUR COMPANY."—*Handbook of Etiquette.*

Mrs. Clovermead. "AND, DAN, YOU'LL BRING THE TRAP—(*recollecting herself—her fashionable Cousin, from London, is on a Visit at the Farm*)—WE SHALL WANT THE CARRIAGE TO DRIVE INTO THE TOWN AFTER LUNCHEON, DANIEL."

Daniel. "YES, MUM—(*hesitating—he had noticed the correction*)—BE I—(*in a loud whisper*)—BE I TO CHANGE MY TROWSE'S, MUM?"!!

Whoever thinks a faultless piece to see
Thinks what ne'er was, nor is, nor e'er shall be.

Alexander Pope (1688–1744)
Essay on Criticism, Part 2, l.53

> **Call the roller of big cigars,**
> **The muscular one, and bid him whip**
> **In kitchen cups concupiscent curds.**
> **Let the wenches dawdle in such dress**
> **As they are used to wear, and let the boys**
> **Bring flowers in last month's newspapers.**
> **Let be be finale of seem.**
> **The only emperor is the emperor of ice-cream.**

Wallace Stevens (1879–1955)
'The Emperor of Ice-cream' (1923)

A poem should not mean / But be

Archibald MacLeish (1892–1982)
'Ars Poetica' (1926), final line

> *Muß es sein? Es muß sein! Es muß sein!*
> Must it be? It must be! It must be!

Ludwig van Beethoven (1770–1827)
written above the opening bars of his last work,
String Quartet in F major, Opus 135

[HAMLET]
   To be, or not to be; that is the question

William Shakespeare (1564–1616)
Hamlet, 3.1.56

Blest hour! It was a luxury—to be!

Samuel Taylor Coleridge (1772–1834)
'Reflections on having left a place of retirement' (1796),
line 43

[on 'the poor Indian']
To be, contents his natural desire,
He asks no angel's wing, no seraph's fire.

Alexander Pope (1688–1744)
Essay on Man, Epistle 1.3

Esse quam videri.
To be, rather than seem to be.

Motto of the 1st Earl of Winterton (1734–88)

We thinke no greater blisse then suche
To be as be we would,
When blessed none but such as be
The same as be they should.

William Warner (1558?–1609)
Albion's England (1586), Book 10, Chapter 59, Stanza 68

[CHRISSY]
I've always wanted to be somebody, but now I
see I should have been more specific.

Jane Wagner (1935–)
The Search for Signs of Intelligent Life in the Universe (1991)

11

2

Being, as was
obituarial be

If the present tense of *be* signals existence, it's open to English speakers to use the past tense to signal non-existence; and so they do. The usage has actually been around a long time—at first, to describe someone who is dead. The *OED* records an example from around the year 1500 of someone being described as 'late purcer to Kynge Henry that was'—meaning the recently deceased King Henry.

A logical development was then for the expression to be used to describe the 'death' of a previous identity, such as referring to a married woman by her maiden name. So in 1785 we find 'Miss Jenny Harry that was, for she afterwards married', and soon after, Jane Austen writing in *Sense and Sensibility* (1811) of Mr Ferrars' lady—'Miss Steele as was'. The usage can also relate to a male difference in status. Here's John Buchan in *Three Hostages* (1924) talking about a letter 'from Lord Artinswell—Sir Walter Bullivant, as was'. Pseudonyms motivate it too: 'The autobiography of former Sex Pistol John Lydon (Rotten, as was)'.

During the twentieth century any identity change came to attract the expression, whether animate or not. The meaning is now 'formerly known as'. We see it in institutions that changed their name: 'You went to the War Office for a bit didn't you? Ministry of Munitions, as was.' Cities and countries too: 'Beijing (Peking, as was)', 'Zimbabwe (Rhodesia, as was)'.

We see a slightly different obituarial use when the expression *as was* is used elliptically—short for *as it was*: 'I want the bungalow rebuilt exactly as was.' There's a website that explores wine history called *Wine As Was*—as it used to be. And when in 1966 EMI released a disc of Manfred Mann's unissued songs from an earlier period, they called it simply *As Was*—short for 'as he was', or (if we're thinking of the group) 'as they were'. It's a short step from here to the meaning 'has just passed' or 'is just over'. Probably the most famous example is the television review *That Was The Week That Was* (1962–3).

As the usage is already expressing non-existence, it might be thought that a negative form would be pointless. Not so. An online writer, having seen on a Victorian map that a different route had been proposed for a well-known canal, headed his piece: 'The Lullymore canal as wasn't'. An elliptical *that wasn't* became quite common in the later twentieth century. There's the famous children's story/film *The Bear That Wasn't* (1946), about a bear who wakes up after a long period of hibernation to find himself in a modern industrial society that refuses to recognize he's a bear and sets him to work as a human. And in recent weeks I've seen the following headlines:

The hurricane that wasn't
The election issue that wasn't (but should have been)
The goal that wasn't

In each case, the missing element is a noun phrase: 'The goal that wasn't a goal'. But the stylistic effect goes beyond tautology: such sentences convey a note of the unexpected, arising out of an error that has been made. As such, a positive counterpart is unlikely: 'The goal that was'?

Related to this is the way we can remember an event that has been and gone (see Chapter 3 on temporal *be*)—a sort of obituary for an event:

Time was, when television was first invented...

The meaning, 'formerly, in the past', made it a popular choice for nostalgic reflections, in song and poetry. The phrase has turned up in pop-song titles at least three times—by singers Chuck Berry and Hadda Brooks, and US rock band Canned Heat. And it's the title of at least three poems, by Dònall Dempsey, Beau Parke, and Fujiwara no Kiyosuke. Some poets use it repeatedly, such as W. S. Gilbert in 'Eheu fugaces' (in *Songs of a Savoyard*, 1890—an allusion to the title of a Horatian ode, which continues *Eheu fugaces... labuntur anni*, 'Alas, the fleeting years are passing'):

Time was when Love and I were well acquainted;
Time was when we walked ever hand in hand;
A saintly youth, with worldly thought untainted,
None better loved than I in all the land!
Time was, when maidens of the noblest station,
Forsaking even military men,
Would gaze upon me, rapt in adoration—
Ah me, I was a fair young curate then!

3

Time being
temporal be

The meaning of *be* often depends on the kind of expression that accompanies it. Used with *where*, it conveys a notion of place. Used with *when* or *how long*, a temporal meaning comes to the fore. A phrase of time is enough to give the verb such meanings as 'occupy, use up, take, stay', in relation to the period that elapses in the course of an activity or process. It's an ancient usage, with examples from as early as around 1200, in the *Ormulum*, when the writer describes how people were amazed that a priest 'swa lannge wass...att godess all-terr'—'was [=stayed] such a long time at God's altar'.

The expressions range from very general time expressions such as [*be*] *so long* and [*be*] *a long time* to very specific expressions such as [*be*] *thirty days*, or this next example, from Shakespeare's *As You Like It*. Amiens tells Jaques that the Duke 'hath been all this day to look you'—to which Jaques replies, 'And I have been all this day to avoid him.' Modern usage has added a colloquial tone:

It'll be hours before the shop opens.

Won't be a minute.

It's been a long time.

Sentences like these have an idiomatic feel to them.

A true idiom—in the sense that the expression has a fixed, unvarying structure—is seen in *for the time being*. This is first recorded in 1449, and judging by the number of *OED* citations—three within twenty years—it quickly became popular, usually with the article, but sometimes without: *for time being*. Its usefulness is suggested by the administrative contexts in which it was used: someone is said to hold a particular office *for the time being*—'during the period under consideration', and often implying 'until some other arrangement is made'. It gradually lost its official resonance, and came to be used in relation to any event that had a temporary status: 'You can stay with us for the time being.' The sense is 'for the present, for now'.

A colloquially shortened form probably developed early on, but examples aren't recorded until the nineteenth century, when novelists were taking pains to represent everyday conversation as faithfully as possible. In Mark Twain's *Life on the Mississippi* (1883), an undertaker expounds the benefits of his trade. When you're embalming a corpse, he says, people will always go for the more expensive option:

It's human nature—human nature in grief. It don't reason, you see. 'Time being, it don't care a dam.

Another temporal idiom is [*to have*] *been and gone*—said of something noteworthy that has both begun and ended. *OED* citations are all from the twentieth century, starting with one from *The Times* in 1911:

Now that the King's review of the Boy Scouts has been and gone.

There's often a hint of disparagement or gloom:

> New Labour has been and gone, and I can't say I'm sorry.
> July has been and gone, and my computer still isn't fixed!

The obituary column for the online BBC magazine is headed 'Been and Gone' (see also Chapter 2 on obituarial *be*).

Some temporal *be*-idioms are no more, in standard English. How do we nowadays refer to previous Mondays? 'Monday last. The Monday before last. Two Mondays ago. Three weeks ago last Monday...' In the fifteenth century, a more succinct expression emerged, which could apply to any specific period of time:

> Monday was a week. [= on the Monday a week before last Monday]
> Monday was a fortnight. [= on the Monday a fortnight before last Monday]
> Monday was three weeks. [= on the Monday three weeks before last Monday]

Some real examples from times past, as recorded by the *OED*:

> 1684: I have been at no Church since August was Twelvemonth.
> 1691: [he] went from his House about last Christmas was 4 years.
> 1772: I arrived here yesterday was a Week.

The *was* is often omitted:

> I was in London Monday three weeks.

In Maria Edgeworth's *The Absentee* (1833), the expression is hyphenated:

> his mistress was in her bed since Thursday-was-a-week

Some quite complex constructions arose, whose interpretation now requires some effort. What does 'On the evening of Saturday was sennight before the day fixed' mean? 'On the evening of the Saturday a week earlier than the Saturday before the day fixed.'

The construction may have died out in standard English, but it was alive and well in some regional dialects during the twentieth century, and probably still is. 'I never left my own parish till Tuesday was a week,' says Christy in J. M. Synge's *The Playboy of the Western World* (1907). And the *OED* has a similar example ('yesterday was a week') from a Pamela Haines novel, *The Kissing Gate*. That was as recently as 1981.

The imperative form: be

*B*E-FORMS have always been associated with the imperative—the verb form used typically to command or instruct. Three instances occur in quick succession in Maureen's advice to Donna in Mike Leigh's *Naked* (1993): 'Be good. If you can't be good, be careful!' The catch-phrase has a long history, starting life in a music-hall song by George Leybourne, whose chorus was one of the most popular beer-hall songs of the 1870s (see also Chapter 23 on musical *be*):

My Mother said, you never should
Walk with a young man through the wood
If you should, do be good, and if you can't, be careful.

Imperative *be* can be negated, expressing a command *not* to do something, as in innumerable modern mantras: 'Don't be evil', 'Don't be good, be great'.

This function of the verb had several early regional variants in Old and Middle English, such as *bia*, *beo*, *bo*, and *bes*. There was a plural form too, seen in Old English *bioð* and *beoð*, with -*th*-forms continuing into Middle English: *beeth*, *beoth*, *beth*. In the north of England they used -*s*, as in *beis* and *bes*. But from the seventeenth century on we find only *be* in standard English for both singular and plural.

There was just one exception to the use of *be* as an imperative: the use of a form resembling *was*. In the West Saxon Gospels, the angel greets Mary in Luke 1.28 with the words 'Hal wes ðu' ('Hail be to you'—the vowel is long: 'hahl'). The usage died out in Middle English, but it is remembered today in a single word. The Old English drinking acclamation to an individual was the singular *wes hal* 'be in good health', and to the whole assembly the plural *wesað hale*. Today: *wassail*.

In the negative, *don't be* has replaced earlier *be not*. In Shakespeare's *Twelfth Night*, Malvolio reads in a letter: 'Be not afraid of greatness'. In the seventeenth century we see the negative particle affixed in such forms as *ben't*, *binna*, and *bissent*, and this continues in modern regional dialects. A 1643 source has 'ben't afraid'; a 1983 Scots version of the Bible has 'binna feared'. There's just a single example recorded in the *OED* of an imperative where both the negative particle and a pronoun are attached—the equivalent of 'don't you be'. It's from Cornwall: *beintee*.

Young children can find imperative *be* somewhat confusing because a similar syllable appears at the beginning of many words in English, as in *believe* and *become*. This has a completely different historical origin, with no relationship to the verb *be*; but little ones don't know this, so we get some lovely examples in reports on language acquisition, such as this one from Ann M. Peters' *The Units of Language Acquisition* (1983; the slant lines enclose a pronunciation using the International Phonetic Alphabet):

Parent: Behave!
Child: But I *am* /heɪv/.

[SECOND APPARITION, *to Macbeth*]
Be bloody, bold, and resolute; laugh to scorn
The power of man; for none of woman born
Shall harm Macbeth.

William Shakespeare (1564–1616)
Macbeth, 4.1.78

Death, be not proud, though some have called
    thee
Mighty and dreadful, for thou art not so;

John Donne (1571–1631)
Holy Sonnets (1633), 10

[POLONIUS]
Neither a borrower nor a lender be,
For loan oft loses both itself and friend,
And borrowing dulleth edge of husbandry.
This above all: to thine own self be true,
And it must follow, as the night the day,
Thou canst not then be false to any man.

William Shakespeare (1564–1616)
Hamlet, 1.13.75

[*Basil Hallward to Dorian Gray*] Don't shrug
    your shoulders like that. Don't be so
    indifferent. You have a wonderful influence.
    Let it be for good, not for evil.

Oscar Wilde (1854–1900)
The Picture of Dorian Gray (1890), Chapter 12

A time being is someone who lives in time,
    and that means you, and me, and every one
    of us who is, or was, or ever will be.

Ruth Ozeki, *A Tale for the Time Being* (2013), Chapter 1

4

Business is business
identifying *be*

One of the most basic uses of *be* is to identify someone or something, or to assert an identity. 'I am David Crystal.' 'They are musicians.' 'John was the first to arrive on the scene.' 'The start time is six o'clock.' 'Happiness is a warm blanket' (Charlie Brown). As the *OED* definition puts it: 'To exist as the person or thing known by a certain name or term; to coincide in identity with, to be identical with'. That seems to sum it up. What more is there to say?

Quite a lot, when we look at the various ways in which this definition works out in practice. The philosophical analysis of *be* has attracted a huge amount of debate as part of a tradition of enquiry into the nature of being, or essence, that began in ancient Greece. Controversy focuses on just how many different functions of *be* there are, and how they are to be precisely distinguished from each other.

A common strategy is to take a grammatical construction using *be* and distinguish the way the verb points us in different semantic directions, depending on the accompanying words. For example, each of the following four sentences has the same grammatical analysis—

Subject + Copula Verb + Complement—but semantically they are very different:

> New York is large. [I'm ascribing a property, or attribute, to New York.]
> New York is a city. [I'm specifying what sort of entity New York is.]
> New York is that large dot on the map. [I'm identifying where New York is.]
> New York is The Big Apple. [I'm equating the two names.]

Not all sentences fall neatly into these four categories. If I say 'New York is exciting', is this a property or a specification, or is it something else, such as an evaluation? We might therefore wish to extend the classification, or conflate some of the categories into a more general one, or introduce subdivisions—recognizing different kinds of identity, for instance. A huge philosophical and semantic literature is devoted to such questions. The range of uses of *be* is truly vast, as the various chapters of this book illustrate, and devising a well-grounded semantic classification that can handle all of them remains a challenge.

My approach in this book is linked to lexicography, rather than to logic or philosophy, and takes the *OED* definitions as a starting-point. One day these definitions will benefit from the systematicity, comprehensiveness, and precision that, in principle, semantic theory can provide; but for entries as complex as *be* that day is still some way off. For the present, I have to make do with semantic observations that are less systematic in character—though I hope still illuminating—relating them where possible to other domains of linguistic enquiry, such as phonology, stylistics, sociolinguistics, and especially grammar.

The examples of identifying *be* in my opening paragraph permit the full range of normal grammatical operations, as the following Shakespearean quotations illustrate. The identity can be stated, as above, or questioned, or commanded, both positively and negatively:

Am I Dromio? Am I your man? Am I myself?   (*The Comedy of Errors*)

[Iago to Othello] Good sir, be a man.   (*Othello*)

[York to Richard] Be not thyself.   (*Richard II*)

The identity can be recent past, distant past, or some time in the future:

[Jaques of Touchstone] A worthy fool: one that hath been a courtier.   (*As You Like It*)

[Helena of Hermia] She was a vixen when she went to school. (*A Midsummer Night's Dream*)

[Macbeth to Banquo] Your children shall be kings.   (*Macbeth*)

The identity is reversible:

[Launce] I am the dog. No, the dog is himself, and I am the dog. O, the dog is me, and I am myself.   (*The Two Gentlemen of Verona*)

And more than one entity can be involved:

A good heart, Kate, is the sun and the moon.   (*Henry V*)

In all these cases, the words on either side of the *be* form are different, which is what we would expect. It would be unusual to find the *be*-form linking the same words. But it happens; and when it does, we know that something else, semantically, is going on.

'Business is business.' When we hear someone say that, we know that this is not intended as a tautology. The speaker is asserting that, when it comes down to commercial matters, it's money that counts; other factors, such as friendship, kinship, and sentimental attachment, are irrelevant. The usage is recorded from the end of the eighteenth century, and it is by no means alone. The general meaning of the construction is that the speaker is emphasizing the nature of the entity being referred to, or affirming its worth, as in the first recorded usage, from 1565:

Truth is truth, and God is God, whether any Councell will or nill.

Often a critical or negative factor is implied. The soldier who says 'War is war' is acknowledging a regrettably necessary event that has just taken place. The tourist who says 'Spain is Spain' has been reporting an uncomfortable experience. The group of friends who agree that 'Jimmy is Jimmy' are making allowances for Jimmy's bad behaviour. And the many literary quotations almost always display an associated note of concession:

A man's a man for a' that.   (Robert Burns, 'Is There for Honest Poverty', 1795)

A book's a book, although there's nothing in't.   (Lord Byron, *English Bards and Scotch Reviewers*, 1816)

Truth is truth howe'er it strike.   (Robert Browning, *La Saisiaz*, 1878)

Some instances have become so familiar that they have achieved the status of proverbs or quotations, 'as sure as eggs is eggs'. The first recorded source for this expression is in 1638: 'They are as like your own, as an egge to an egge'. 'As sure as eggs be eggs', meaning 'with great certainty', appears before the end of the seventeenth century. And then, in Thomas Hughes' *Tom Brown's School Days* (1857) we see Tom coming out with the present-day usage:

I shall come out bottom of the form, as sure as eggs is eggs.

Brewer's Dictionary of Phrase and Fable suggests the expression is an adaptation of the logician's 'x = x'. That's always a possibility, I suppose, but I think the visual identity between eggs is a much more likely source for such an everyday expression. And the lack of standard English agreement between subject and verb hasn't stopped it from achieving widespread currency, alongside the more formal 'eggs are eggs'.

Another unexpected usage is when the *be*-form is strongly stressed. It's unusual because identity hardly seems to be something that needs emphasis—apart from the obvious cases where someone has just queried it. I would only ever say 'The time *is* six o'clock' if someone had just expressed some doubt about the matter. But there are many interesting cases where we find an emphatic form without any hint of a doubt or contradiction in the preceding context:

For many years, Noam Chomsky *was* linguistics.
The internet *is* the future.

Examples of this kind are affirming an identity in essence, not in literal fact. The entity before the verb is being thought of as the embodiment or expression of the entity after the verb. It's a fairly recent usage, with recorded instances no earlier than the eighteenth century, but it's popular today—especially in tabloid circles, where the role of a football manager, for example, is lauded in that way, as in this online header in 2015:

Arsene Wenger *is* Arsenal, so what happens when he leaves?

The usage allows the negative too, as in another online header:

Online gaming isn't the future; it's the present.

And, to complete the time possibilities, we have this one:

Why MultiWindow *was* the Past, *is* the Present and *will be* the Future.

Finally, in relation to the identifying function of *be*, note the case of temporary identity, as when someone takes a part in a film or play:

I am Horatio in the next production.
Mary was a fantastic Lady Macbeth.
Jim will be a great Macbeth.

The identification may be reversed, as when a radio announcer lists actors' names before a play. Now the *is* means 'is being played by':

Hamlet is John Brown.
Ophelia is Mary Smith.

These are everyday examples, reported a thousand times in announcements and reviews. But how are we to take an example like the following?

Benedict Cumberbatch *is* Sherlock Holmes.

This can hardly be an announcement, as he has become well known for playing the role. Rather, it has to be another instance of the affirmation of essence: the writer is saying Cumberbatch is the true embodiment of Sherlock Holmes. That move, from identification to confirmation, is something all actors hope to achieve. Or, in linguistic terms, the move from an unstressed to a stressed form of *be*.

5

I am to resign
obligational *be*

When *be* is followed by an infinitive, it often expresses obligation or necessity. If chairman John returns to his office after a board meeting and announces 'I am to resign', the implication is that he has no choice in the matter, that circumstances have put him in this position. It may be his duty to resign, or it may be simply an appropriate course of action. Whatever the factors, he understands that he has to go.

This usage has been in the language since Anglo-Saxon times. Here are some literary examples from the eighteenth and nineteenth centuries. In Samuel Richardson's *Pamela* (1741), we see the writer using the verb to express social appropriateness:

I am to thank you, my dear Miss, for your kind Letter.

In one of Thackeray's letters (1839), we see it expressing the inevitability of an impending event:

There is to be penny postage … in 10 days.

In *The Water-babies* (1863), Charles Kingsley teases the reader with a mock command:

Don't you know that this is a fairy tale, and all fun and pretence; and
that you are not to believe one word of it, even if it is true?

And this obligational sense is the dominant one today:

I am to take the tablets three times a day.
We are to go by bus after all.

In such examples, the verb + particle 'to' can be replaced by 'have to'.

A related usage is found when the infinitive form of the verb is in
the passive, as in these examples:

The play is to be performed in period costume.
Joan is to be married tomorrow.
The country was to be attacked in two waves.
I passed a shop where any article was to be had for a pound.

Here the necessity is not so much one of obligation as of organization:
the event will happen, because it is the outcome of some planning. It
is 'to be expected'.

1st person singular, present tense, indicative mood: I am

J UDGING by the spellings, this form had a variety of pronunciations in Old English dialects. We see it as *æm*,
am, and *amm*, especially in the Midlands and North, presumably sounding very much like the way we say it today.
But spellings such as *eam*, *eom*, and *æom* were also very frequent, especially in the South. These suggest a pronunciation

as a diphthong, starting with a strong vowel like that of the *e* in *get*, and followed by a weaker vowel which would probably have been like the vowel of *the*. The *eom* form was important in West Saxon—the dialect that comes closest to being a standard—and is the one most often shown in grammars of Old English.

An *emme* spelling in Middle English suggests that some speakers said the word with the vowel of *get*. Some must also have pronounced it with an initial puff of aspiration, judging by the spellings *heom*, *hamme*, and *ham*, which are noticeable during that period—a feature that stayed in Cockney speech. Among the interesting later regional variants, in the eighteenth and nineteenth centuries, are those that add an *-s* (*ams*) and those carrying over the end of the pronoun *I* (*yam*)—a form made famous by cartoon character Popeye's 'I yam what I yam'. Several vowel variations are seen, such as a lengthened version *aam* in Ireland, and *im* and *um* in Northern England.

At the same time, many regions—again, chiefly in the Midlands and North—used a form based on *be* for the 1st person, both with a final *m* (*beam*, *beom*, *bium*) and without (*beo*, *be*, *bee*). Forms ending in *n* appear in Middle English, and continue into the eighteenth century: *beon*, *byn*, *bin*, *bene*. From the nineteenth century, recorded forms in Southern England, Ireland, and the US South (especially in African-American dialects) show a final *s*: *bees*, *bes*, *be's*. Subtle shifts of meaning are sometimes present. A dialect might contain both *I am* and *I be*, with the latter conveying a habitual meaning: *I am a farmer* vs *I be at the market every Thursday*.

In Northern England and Scotland, the 1st person was often expressed by the *is* form, spelled variously (*is, es, as, iz, yiz*), and this became especially heard in regional speech in the southern USA and the Caribbean. These parts of the world, in the nineteenth century, also show *are* and *ar*. That usage is still around, coexisting with other forms, as in this line from *Rehab*, by hip-hop artist Lecrae: 'I'm who I are, a trail of stardust leading to the superstar'.

Representations of regional speech, from Middle English on, also show forms in which the old form of the 1st person pronoun, *ic* (pronounced 'itch'), is attached to the verb: *icham, ycham*, with the vowel often dropped (*cham, 'cham*). In the opening scene of Ben Jonson's *The Tale of a Tub* (published in 1640), Squire Tub's man, Basket-Hilts, is given a marked rural accent, and uses two such forms in his first speech: 'Ich'am no zive [sieve], Cham no mans wife'.

Virtually all the above forms turn up contracted, with examples recorded from the sixteenth century. Alongside *I'm*, which became the modern informal standard form, we see *I're* (from *I are*) and *I'se* (from *I is*), along with several spelling variations, such as *I'z*. The negative form also varies greatly. In Old English we see the negation prefixed to the *am*: *I neam, næm, nam*—a usage that lasts well into the sixteenth century. Then it moves to the end, with *amn't, amna, amnae, ammot, am't*, and many other variations. At the same time, from the sixteenth century on, we see forms dropping the *m* appear—first *an't*, then *ain't*, again with many regional variants such as *een't* in Suffolk, *yunt* in Worcestershire, *yent* in Berkshire, *ant* in New England, and *ent* in African-American usage.

Today, *ain't* is considered non-standard, but it's widespread throughout the English-speaking world—probably used far more often than the standard equivalent—and a century ago it was actually acceptable upper-class speech, turning up frequently in the novels of the period. Here's the lawyer Mr Wharton arguing with his sister-in-law over his daughter's future, in Anthony Trollope's *The Prime Minister* (1875): 'I ain't thinking of her marrying'. And towards the end of the novel the Duke of Omnium himself asks someone: 'I hope you ain't cold'.

All the other positive variants appear with negative counterparts, with usages recorded from the sixteenth century on. Based on *be*, the many alternatives include *bee'nt*, *ben't*, *been't*, *bain't*, *byunt*, *binna*, and *bisn't*. Based on *is*: *isn't*, *izn't*, *izzant*, *inna*, *idn't*, and *in't*. Based on *are*: *aren't*, *arn't*, *ar'na*, and *arem't*. This led to the curious situation where *I aren't* is considered non-standard, but *I'm ready, aren't I?* is standard. Not everyone liked it, when it first came in. The *OED* has a quotation from Lady Grove's *The Social Fetich* (1907): 'If "ain't I?" is objected to, surely "aren't I?" is very much worse'.

The huge number of negative variants suggest that English speakers have never been totally comfortable with the irregularity of the 1st person form. It is indeed the odd-one-out in standard English, when compared to the way the other persons express negation. We can say happily:

he/she/it is > he/she/it isn't > is he/she/it? > isn't he/she/it?
we/you/they are > we/you/they aren't > are we/you/they? >
    aren't we/you/they?

but the 1st person gives learners two problems:

I am > I'm not (*not* I amn't) > am I? > aren't I? (*not* amn't I?)

It's a weird situation: the statement form uses *am*, but doesn't allow a *not*-contraction; the negative question form uses *are* and does allow a *not*-contraction. The logical course would have been to allow *amn't* in, to make the set regular; but language has never been governed by logic, and it's not clear historically why the 1st person moved in these different directions in standard English. Perhaps the use of *amn't* in some regional dialects, such as Scottish and Irish English, had something to do with it.

"Bobbie, you must not say that word"
"Daddy does."
"Yes; but Daddy's Daddy."
"Well, I'm I'm."

I am! yet what I am none cares or knows,
My friends forsake me, like a memory lost.

John Clare (1793–1864)
'I am', written while in a lunatic asylum (published 1848)

> [IAGO, *to Roderigo*]
> For when my outward action doth demonstrate
> The native act and figure of my heart
> In compliment extern, 'tis not long after
> But I will wear my heart upon my sleeve
> For daws to peck at; I am not what I am.

William Shakespeare (1564–1616)
Othello, 1.1.62

And God said unto Moses: I am that I am.

Exodus 3.14

> I think, therefore I am. [*Ego cogito, ergo sum.*]

René Descartes (1596–1650)
Principia Philosophiae [Principles of Philosophy] (1644),
part 1, article 7

NUMBER SIX: Who are you?
NUMBER TWO: The new Number Two.
NUMBER SIX: Who is Number One?
NUMBER TWO: You are Number Six.
NUMBER SIX: I am not a number! I am a free
    man!

The Prisoner (ITV, 1967), Introduction

6

Has the doctor been?
visitational *be*

During the second half of the eighteenth century—there are as yet no earlier citations—a new use of *be* developed. In the form *has/have/had been*, and followed by the preposition *to* before a noun phrase, it took on the meaning of 'gone to visit' a place. Two examples from Fanny Burney's novel *Evelina* (1778):

> We have been to the opera, and I am still more pleased than I was on Tuesday.
>
> I have been to Berry Hill, and there I had my intelligence, and, at the same time, the unwelcome information of your ill health.

Forms such as *have been* show that the event being talked about is recent, or felt to be so. The speaker has visited and returned, and the event is still very much in mind. Linguists talk about it having 'current relevance'. We can imagine a *just* being added, as in this example from a T. S. Eliot letter in 1915:

> I have just been to a cubist tea.

It's a reporter's usage, and so it turns up a lot in official statements of recent activities. What did the King do yesterday? The *Westminster Gazette* in 1902 reports:

His Majesty has been to Westminster Abbey, and the Crystal Palace…

It thus tends to be often used when talking about special events, when someone makes a visit in order to be present at a special occasion.

In earlier English, the past tense was used in a similar way, resulting in a sequence of tenses that can confuse the modern reader, as in this letter, written by Lady Shaftesbury in 1747, telling her addressee of her recent outings:

The last opera (or rather the scenery) is, I find, very much admired by the generality of the town, but I am so unfashionable as not to have been yet to see it. I was to see the new farce, which I think has neither wit nor spirit, but its merit consists in the representation…

The context makes it perfectly clear that she *has* seen the new farce, whereas today the 'was to' construction could only mean that something had stopped her from seeing it. Nowadays, I've encountered such a usage only in Irish English: 'I was to buy some meat this morning'. Is it more widespread regionally, I wonder?

The important factor is current relevance. This allows the visitational sense to be used of indefinite past time, as in 'Have you been to Australia?', where we could add *ever* (and not *just*). We have to see such a sentence in context to see the relevance of the remark:

John: I went to visit my brother in Australia last month. Have you ever been…?
Mary: Yes, I have.

Here, the aim is to compare experiences. It doesn't matter when Mary was in Australia; the important point is that John wants to ask her something that bears on his own visit.

During the twentieth century, it was increasingly common to see the verb used without the prepositional phrase. Usually, the visit is related to an occupation: the person has come and gone professionally. The location is taken for granted. In examples like these, something like 'to the house' is understood:

Has the doctor been to-day?

The postman hasn't been yet.

The health visitor's been.

The gardeners have been.

You can tell my daughter and her dogs have been.

A similar example is when the visitor has some sort of expected status, as in hospital visiting:

Have you had any visitors today, Mrs Jones?

Yes, my husband's been.

It's a usage that children encounter quite early in life, as on Christmas morning:

Santa's been!

We're unlikely to use it for unexpected or unwelcome visitors. In talking about a burglary to a neighbour, we could easily say 'The police have been'. But would we ever say 'The burglars have been'? I suppose, if it was a regular occurrence...

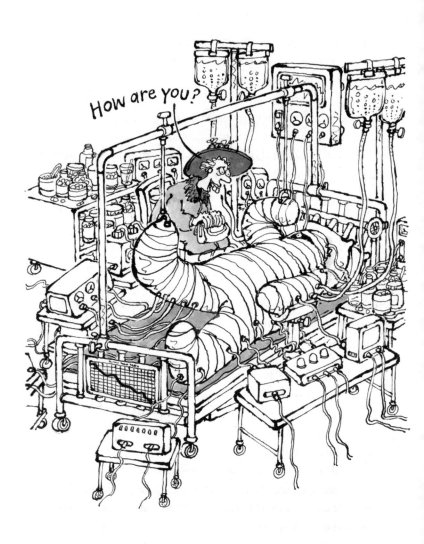

7

How are you?
circumstantial *be*

Be is the default verb when we want to express the idea of being in a particular condition, as when we make a general enquiry about health or the weather. 'How are you?' 'I'm well.' The sense is: 'What state are you in right now?' 'I'm in the state of being well.' The usage resembles the general meaning of *be* when it expresses existence (see Chapter 1), but now we're talking about a situation constrained by the circumstances of a particular time and place. If I phone and ask you 'What's the weather like?', I'm not expecting an existential account of the nature of weather by way of reply. I'm expecting simply 'It's fine' or 'It's awful'. And if I sensed any possible ambiguity, I could have added an adverbial like *today* or *now* to my question.

It's another very old usage, recorded since Anglo-Saxon times. People have always wanted to talk about their state of mind or body or the situation they are in: 'She is too cautious', 'I'm not at ease', 'You are in some trouble'. Abstract notions are affected too: 'Proposals are being discussed', 'The victory is ours'.

These are all real states: they *are* taking place. The same use of *be* is found when we want to talk about unreal or hypothetical states—states that *could* exist. We see it in idioms like *be that as it may*, which has a few variations in earlier usage, such as *be it as it may* and *be this as it may*. Touchstone, in Shakespeare's *As You Like It*, spells out the second verb when he reflects on Audrey, his future wife:

> Well, praised be the gods for thy foulness; sluttishness may come here-after. But be it as it may be, I will marry thee.

A modern colloquial variant is *that's as may be*—though this expresses a stronger sense of reservation. *Be that as it may* can usually be glossed as an unemphatic 'all the same'. With *that's as may be*, what is about to be said is *much* more important than what has just been said.

As it were is another hypothetical idiom, expressing the notion of 'if one might so put it' or 'in a manner of speaking'. It's first recorded in early Middle English, and is a usage that people employ when they're moving outside their linguistic comfort zone. When Sir Humphry Davy, writing about agricultural chemistry, says 'It is necessary from time to time to change, and as it were to cross the breed', he's adopting a metaphor that isn't part of his normal manner of discourse, but which he hopes will better convey what he has in mind. When Edmund Burke writes in a letter that the government 'as it were have a bird's eye view of everything', he knows he is being approximate, and the phrase in effect asks his listener to make allowances and not take the metaphor too literally.

Another such idiom is *were it not for* or, more explicitly, *if it were not for*, where the intention is to express an exception to a state of affairs:

> Were it not for the noise, I would have given the hotel five stars.
> If it were not for social media, I don't know how I'd be able to keep in touch.

The *were* form keeps the time pointing backwards, to events that *have* taken place and which may still have current relevance. The idiom can move a stage further back in time: 'had it not been for the noise', 'if it had not been for the noise'. But there isn't a future form: 'if it will not be for the noise'. To express possibilities about things that haven't happened yet, English provides the *if*-construction using *were* or (from the eighteenth century) *was*, the difference today being largely a matter of style or regional dialect:

If she were to leave, the company would be in difficulty.
If she was to leave, the company would be in difficulty.

The *were* form is more formal.

There have been other ways of expressing future uncertainty with *be*, but they seem to be largely obsolete—or, as the *OED* puts it, 'somewhat literary'. Do people still use *good/better/best* followed by an infinitive, but without the *to*? Such constructions once were very common, as in these Shakespeare instances:

[Hamlet, of the players] After your death you were better have a bad
   epitaph than their ill report while you live.   (*Hamlet*)
[Iago tells Othello] You were best go in.   (*Othello*)

The latest recorded instance in the *OED* of *good* used in this way is from a long time ago—1789, in a travel journal by Hester Lynch Piozzi:

It were as good live at Brest or Portsmouth...as here.

Constructions such as 'It were better be sure than sorry' and 'You were best stay here' can still be heard in regional dialects; but standard British English prefers to rephrase, using *to*, such as 'It will be better to be sure than sorry' and 'It would be best if you were to stay here'.

And does anyone still say *what one would be at*, meaning 'what one aims at', 'what one has in mind'? That construction is recorded from the late sixteenth century:

[when witches meet in churches] at what time their master enquiring at them what they would be at: everie one of them propones unto, what wicked turne they would have done.　(James VI of Scotland, *Daemonologie*, 1597, Chapter 5)

The love of girls is uncertain, capricious, and so foolish that we cannot always discover what the young lady would be at; nay, it may almost be doubted whether she always knows this herself.　(Henry Fielding, *Tom Jones*, 1749)

[Charles' wife, trying to get her point across] all that is very true; but not what I would be at.　(Oliver Goldsmith, *The Vicar of Wakefield*, 1769)

What would revolutionising Germany be at?　(*Blackwood's Edinburgh Magazine*, 1848)

It seems to have gone from standard English, but regional dialects have a habit of holding on to constructions that the standard rejects, often with a different sense. Today, when I hear it, it means 'What are you doing?' or 'What are you up to?' In Newfoundland, it turns up in shortened form: 'You at?' And an angry Irish tweet during the 2015 Rugby World Cup cursed the Irish side for their play: 'What are they at?' The rest of the tweet was unprintable.

8

I've been with someone
sexual *be*

For centuries, a sentence such as *I've been with someone* could only have had an innocent, traveller meaning, with the geographical destination known from the previous context. But during the early nineteenth century, judging by the earliest *OED* citations, an 'absolute' use of the construction emerged, in which there was no destination—at least not in the usual sense of the word. *To have been with* developed the meaning of 'to have had sexual intercourse with'.

It was a euphemism that well suited the Victorian era because its ambiguity conveyed a sense of mystery. It allowed people to allude to the unmentionable, while giving their listeners the option of choosing a weaker interpretation if they so wished. When they saw such a sentence as 'he said she had been with another man' (in the *Annual Register* for 1855), they could accept the sexual reading or choose to ignore it, imagining the sentence to convey such polite meanings as 'she was accompanied by'.

As time went by, the contexts became more explicit. There's no real chance of ambiguity when we read, in one of the tales recounted by

George Dorsey in *The Mythology of the Wichita* (1804), that 'the oldest brother began to tell the rest how he had been with a woman for the first time in his life'. And there's definitely no ambiguity with later twentieth-century citations:

1959: He hadn't been with a woman in over a year.

1993: My assumption is that I haven't been with a risk case.

Nor is there any likelihood of misunderstanding when the context is totally clear, as when a guidance manual on sexually transmitted diseases, written in dialogue form, asks the reader: 'Does this mean my partner has been with someone else?' But in less obvious situations, the uncertainty can come to the surface, as in this snippet of dialogue from Jessie McClain's novel *My Dearest Rose* (2011).

'I was just wondering whether you have ever been with anybody?' he asks.

I stare at him as he does me. It looks as if he's bracing himself for my reaction.

'Do you mean *been with* the way I think you mean *been with*?' I ask, trying to stifle a laugh.

As with *been and gone and done it*, the usage is chiefly encountered in the perfective form, where *have* combines with *be*. A sentence like *Have you been with someone?* prioritizes the sexual sense—a sense that is far less dominant in *Are you with someone?* or *Will you be with someone?* The usage remains popular, probably because of its succinctness—much shorter than the other locutions, such as *been sleeping with* or *gone to bed with*.

Is it fair to ask an ex if she's been with anyone if you're considering getting back together?

And today after he's been with somebody else, he snapchats me 'I love you'.

I'm a guy that has never been with anybody outside my race.

These are rhythmically punchier than the alternatives, less formal than the dictionary definition ('have sexual intercourse with'), and far more polite than the down-to-earth options (such as replacing *with* by *fucking*).

The expression is time-sensitive. A specific temporal phrase of long duration immediately downgrades the sexual meaning:

I've been with my boyfriend for six weeks.

That surely has to mean 'I've been going out with my boyfriend' over that time—though I suppose, with a bit of imagination, you could just about read in a sense of habitual action.

2nd person singular, present tense, indicative mood: you are

SIGNS of the extraordinary dialectal future of this form of the verb appear very early in the history of English. The opening words of the Lord's Prayer in its usual modern form are 'Our father, which art in heaven'. In the Mercian dialect of Old English, in the Rushworth Gospels, we see it as

fæder ure þu þe in heofunum *earð*
fæder ure þu þe *eart* on heofonum

In the Northumbrian dialect, in the Lindisfarne Gospels, it also appears in two forms:

fader ure ðu *arð* in heofnum
fader ure ðu *bist* in heofnum

In the West Saxon dialect, which eventually became the norm for Old English, we see it spelled as *art*, and this is the form that later comes to dominate. Local pronunciations continue to be seen in such spellings as *erte*, *at*, and *yarth*, and there is an intriguing cluster in Middle English, suggesting that some speakers said the word with an initial [h], as in *hart* and *hert*. But *art* became the standard form.

Alongside *thou art* we see *thou are*—far less common, but in steady use down the centuries, and with a similar range of local pronunciations. I wasn't expecting to see it in anything modern, but the lexicographers tracked one down in the twenty-first century. Barbara Morris, in her anti-aging book *Put Old on Hold* (2003), adopts a mock-religious style for her set of commandments, and one runs like this:

> If thou are a woman over 50, thou certainly shall not have a relationship with a younger man *unless* thou are a celebrity.

There are several other instances in the chapter. It's a curious mixture of ancient and modern.

Since the seventeenth century, *you are* has become the only accepted form for the second person singular in standard English. Speakers and writers of that variety only encounter *thou art* in a small range of distinctive settings, such as prayers, the Bible, Shakespeare, and imaginative reconstructions of the speech of such characters as Robin Hood, King Arthur, variegated pirates, and the medieval heroes of innumerable children's comics.

In regional dialects, *thou/you art/are* is in competition with several other popular forms. One group clusters around variants of *be*. There was an example in the Northumbrian 'Our Father' above, and along with *bist* we find such forms as *bees*, *beest*, *beost*, and *bes*, as well as *been*, *ben*, and *beth*. Often there's a contrast in meaning, with *are/art* conveying a one-off event, and forms based on *be* used for a habitual activity:

thou art a coward—from the way you're behaving now
thou be a coward—you always act in a cowardly way
you are on the ferry—I can see you are
you be on the ferry—you work on board a ferry

In the north of England and in Scotland, people said *thou is* and *you is*, and this usage turns up in various parts of the English-speaking world, especially in the Caribbean and the American South. Here's an example from Charles C. Jones' *Negro Myths from the Georgia Coast, told in the vernacular* (1888):

One day eh meet Buh Rabbit in de big road, an eh ax um how eh mek out fur water. Buh Rabbit say him no casion fuh hunt water: him lib off de jew on de grass. Buh Wolf quire: 'Enty you blan tek water outer me spring?' Buh Rabbit say: 'Me yent.' Buh Wolf say: 'You yis. Enty me see you trak?'

Brer Rabbit gets out of it by claiming the tracks belong to some other rabbit.

Another Southern regionalism for this form of the verb is *you em* or *am*. It seems that any form of the verb *be* can be used as the 2nd person: *thou/you am, are/art, is*. And the same diversity appears in the regional variants when abbreviated. We see such forms as *you'm, thou'rt, thou're, thou's,* and *you's* alongside the modern informal standard *you're*. Novelists in particular like to show the colloquial pronunciation: 'Yer the lowest of the low, you are,' shouts Flo, in Annie Murray's *The Narrowboat Girl* (2001). And Izz in Thomas Hardy's *Tess of the d'Urbervilles* (1891) asks 'B'you awake, Tess?' Sometimes it's the pronoun that is abbreviated: *th'art, t'art, y'are*. And the dialect literature is full of question-forms where a shortened form of the pronoun comes after the verb, as in *artou, arta, bistu,* and *bista*. 'Arta mad?' 'Bista coming?'

A whole new set of forms express what in standard English since the eighteenth century appears as *aren't/are not*. In Old and Middle English we see *nart, n'art,* and *nert*—in early Middle English sometimes with the pronoun attached: *nartu, nertu*. The variations grow after the sixteenth century: *arn't, are'nt, ar'n't, an't,* in Scotland *arnae* and *arna,* and everywhere—as with the 1st person—*ain't* (Panel on p. 32). Some dialects use forms based on *art: artn't, artna,* and the unusual-looking *atten*. There are some fascinating combinations, such as this one from Tennessee in 1827: 'Thou an't sick, child, art thee?'

Also, during the sixteenth century, we see forms recorded based on *be*. Some simply add the negative particle to the word *be* (in various pronunciations), as in *bent, bain't, binna, byant, beant*. Some add it to *bist* or *be's*, with apostrophes scattered throughout: *beesnt, beestna, bisnt, bistnt, bis'n't, be's'n't*. Some neat parallelisms are recorded: a dialect publication in 1905 has 'Sometimes you be and sometimes you beunt'. From the eighteenth century and after, there are recorded forms based on *is*: *you isn't, i't, in't*.

But the crowning glory of all the distinctive forms for the second person has surely got to be what happened in the nineteenth century to *ain't* followed by a pronoun. The fashion in representing colloquial speech was to show the blending of the final consonant of *ain't* and the initial consonant of *you*, resulting in *aintcha*. It was spelled in all sorts of ways: as well as *aintcha* we find *aincha, ain'tcha, ain't'cha, ain't-cha*, and *aint'cha*. *Aren't you* received the same treatment: *aren'cha, arencha, arentcha, aren'tcha*.

Ain'tcha became famous because it proved to be a particular favourite of singers, such as Helen Kane (remembered for her hit 'I wanna be loved by you') and Frank Sinatra ('Ain'tcha ever coming back'). Here's Kane singing in the 1929 film *Pointed Heels*:

now listen while I say…
Ain'tcha kinda glad, and ain'tcha kinda gay,

> When you hear me say, "I love you,"
> Oh, tell me, baby, ain'tcha?

And—my favourite example—in 'The 59th Street Bridge Song', aka 'Feelin' Groovy', a big hit from Simon and Garfunkel in 1966:

> Hello, lamppost, whatcha knowin'?
> I've come to watch your flowers growin'
> Ain'tcha got no rhymes for me? …

Doo-it, doo-doo, feelin' groovy.

"EVIL COMMUNICATIONS," &c.

Lord Reginald. "AIN'T YER GOIN' TO HAVE SOME PUDDIN', MISS RICHARDS? IT'S SO JOLLY!"

The Governess. "THERE AGAIN, REGINALD! 'PUDDIN' '—'GOIN' '—' AIN'T YER' !!! THAT'S THE WAY JIM BATES AND DOLLY MAPLE SPEAK—AND JIM'S A *STABLE-BOY*, AND DOLLY'S A *LAUNDRY-MAID*!"

Lord Reginald. "AH! BUT THAT'S THE WAY FATHER AND MOTHER SPEAK, *TOO*—AND FATHER'S A *DUKE*, AND MOTHER'S A *DUCHESS*!! SO THERE!"

OLIVIA: I prithee, tell me what thou think'st of me?
VIOLA: That you do think you are not what you are.
OLIVIA: If I think so, I think the same of you.
VIOLA: Then think you right; I am not what I am.
OLIVIA: I would you were as I would have you be.
VIOLA: Would it be better, madam, than I am?

    I wish it might, for now I am your fool.

William Shakespeare (1564–1616)
Twelfth Night, 3.1.135

RICHARD

    Let me put in your minds, if you forget,
    What you have been ere this, and what you are;
    Withal, what I have been, and what I am.
QUEEN MARGARET (*aside*)
    A murderous villain, and so still thou art.

William Shakespeare (1564–1616)
Richard III, 3.1.130

But thou has long had place to prove
This truth—to prove, and make thine own:
'Thou hast been, shalt be, art, alone'.

Matthew Arnold (1822–88)
'Isolation. To Marguerite' (1857), l.29

I'm Nobody! Who are you?
Are you—Nobody—too?
Then there's a pair of us!
Don't tell! they'd advertise—you know!

Emily Dickinson (1830–86)
'I'm Nobody' (1891)

9
Two and two is four
numerical *be*

The most precise context for *be* appears when it is surrounded by numbers. Now it means 'equates to', 'is equal to'. There's a similar use of *make*: 'Two and two makes four'. It's the staple usage in mathematics, introducing the result of a calculation, whether addition, subtraction, multiplication, or division.

Examples have been recorded since the fifteenth century, and they show divided usage. Which is it?

Two and two is four.
Two and two are four.

If we're thinking of the numbers preceding the verb as separate entities, then we're likely to say *are*. But if we're thinking of them as a single formulaic expression (equivalent to 'the sum of two and two'), we're going to say *is*. In the latter case, we can expand the formula indefinitely:

Two plus two minus one times three is...

These examples illustrate the contrast between a unitary and a multiple meaning:

Three times seven is twenty-one.

Three sevens are what I need to win.

And in literature, as opposed to mathematics, we'll find both, with *is/are* and *make/makes*:

Seven mornings a pint at two pence is seven twos is a shilling and twopence over.   (James Joyce, *Ulysses*, 1922)

Freedom is the freedom to say that two plus two make four. (*George Orwell, 1984*, 1949)

For many, the *are* usage has stayed in the mind thanks to Danny Kaye (and many others after him), who sang Frank Loesser's 'Inchworm' song in the 1952 film *Hans Christian Andersen*:

Inchworm, inchworm

(Two and two are four)

Measuring the marigolds

(Four and four are eight)

You and your arithmetic

(Eight and eight are sixteen)

You'll probably go far

(Sixteen and sixteen are thirty-two).

A related use is in the context of money, referring to a calculated value. Now it means 'to cost, to be priced at'. The basic question is 'How much is it?' And the answers cover the whole range of costs, benefits, and commodities:

The price is two euros a piece.
The reward is a thousand dollars.
The bill was thirty pounds.
The tickets are five pence each.

Some monetary uses of *be* have died out. In late Middle English, we find it with the meaning 'be good for' or 'be at the expense of'. Towards the end of Shakespeare's *The Taming of the Shrew*, the men wager whether their wives will come at their bidding. Baptista tells Lucentio:

I'll be your half Bianca comes.

He means: 'I'll go half-shares with you'. And in Henry Fielding's *Tom Jones* (1749), we read:

The wine being now at an end, the barber pressed very eagerly to be his bottle; but Jones absolutely refused, saying 'He had already drank more than he ought'.

The barber wants to stand Tom Jones a drink.

The last recorded usage in the *OED* is in 1865, when George Borrow, visiting an Anglesey inn in *Wild Wales*, is treated to a jug of ale and tries to go halves: 'I must insist on being my share'. At the end of the nineteenth century, Joseph Wright included in his *English Dialect Dictionary* examples of exactly this kind from Ayrshire and Suffolk. That's almost living memory. I wonder if this use of *be* still has some regional life today?

3rd person singular, present tense, indicative mood: he/she/it is

ALTHOUGH *is* has often been used regionally with the 1st person (*I is*) and 2nd person (*you is*), its dominant presence in the history of English has been as the 3rd person singular.

The *i* spelling of the vowel runs through the whole history of the word from Old English to the present day. Variants include *ys* (suggesting a rounded vowel quality, such as we hear today in French *tu*) and forms with *e*, chiefly in the north of England, such as *ese* and *ess*. As with the 1st person, some people must for a time have inserted an initial /h/, for we see such spellings as *hiis*, *hes*, and *hyse* in Middle English. Others must have added a /j/, in view of such spellings as *yis* and *yes*.

The pronunciation of *s* is unusual, at the end of a word like this. Only *as*, *has*, *was*, and *his* are similar in their use of a voiced sound, /z/, where the vocal cords are vibrating. In Old English, letter *s* was regularly used to represent /z/ as well as the voiceless sound /s/, but the pronunciation of *is* seems to have been voiceless, as indicated by such spellings as *ist* and *iss*, and later *isse*. The voiced consonant became the norm during the Middle English period, and remains so today for most English accents. The only non-regional instance of a voiceless consonant after the 3rd person pronoun nowadays is in the contraction *it's*.

Some accents (such as Welsh English) do retain the voiceless sound, often shown as *iss* in dialect writing. Shakespeare shows us another voiceless variant, for Irish English, when in *Henry V* Captain Macmorris laments about the siege of Harfleur:

> By Chrish, la, 'tish ill done! The work ish give over, the trompet sound the retreat. By my hand I swear, and my father's soul, the work ish ill done...

Other accents reflect the /z/. Anyone representing an accent from the West Country of England, for example, is likely to go for a spelling such as *iz* or *uz*, even though that actually doesn't change the pronunciation at all.

Is has always been in competition with *be* for the right to represent the 3rd person singular. Forms such as *bið* and *byð*, with a wide range of spelling variations of the vowel reflecting different accents, are found throughout Old and Middle English. In the north of England we see forms ending in *-s*, such as *bees*, *bes*, and *bez*, and these—again in a variety of spellings—are found in regional writing right through to the present day. There are forms ending in *-n* too, such as *bin*, *bene*, and *beyn*. Examples from British dialects over the past hundred years or so include *it biz* (Northamptonshire), *'e bin* (Shropshire), *it be* (Hertfordshire), *her bist* (Worcestershire), and *she bees* (Ulster). The USA provides many parallel usages. In some dialects, as with the 1st and

2nd person, the forms based on *be* express habitual activity: *she is working* means 'she's working now'; *she bees working* means 'she has a regular job'.

Other variants are also recorded as a 3rd person singular, especially in southern dialects of England, southern USA, and the Caribbean islands: *it are a miracle*; *it am the truth*. None, however, approach the frequency of the forms based on *be*.

For students of English literature, the usage that probably most often attracts attention is the combination of *is* with a preceding reduced form of *it*, to produce *'tis*. There are over 1,400 instances in Shakespeare, for example. The spelling varies, especially in the use of the apostrophe (*t'is*, *ti's*), and often showing no apostrophe at all. In Middle English, the pronoun is sometimes used twice: *as it tis*. This is of course a perfectly normal pronunciation in everyday colloquial speech, in all dialects (including standard English), though in writing it tends to be used as a sign of a regional dialect. And the same point applies to the use of *is* followed by a reduced form of *it*: *is't*, with spelling variants such as *ist* and *i'st*, as well as the reduplicated *ist't*. This is much less frequent in Shakespeare—less than 200 instances. 'Is't possible?' asks Hamlet.

The modern contracted form, *'s*, appears in *he's*, *she's*, and *it's*. In dialects that use *am*, there's also a contracted form: *she'm right*. Representations of colloquial speech often show the contracted form without the pronoun: *'s too bad*. This usage became famous when it was used by George and Ira Gershwin in the musical *Funny Face* (1927):

'S wonderful, 's marvelous
You should care for me
'S awful nice, 's paradise
'S what I love to see.

Here the omitted form is *it*; but the same contraction can be seen with the omission of *that*, as in *'sright* and *'sall there is to it*.

The modern negative form is *isn't*, in standard English. Earlier variants show the negative element preceding, as in *nis* and *nys*. These were dying out at the end of the sixteenth century, but the form is still to be seen, for example, in Edmund Spenser's *Shepherd's Calendar* (1579): *Thou findest faulte where nys to be found* (= 'where it is not'). Since then, the negative element has followed the verb—but with many regional variations, such as *isnae*, *is'n*, and *isna*, as well as a cluster of variants in which /z/ is replaced by /d/, such as *idnt*, *idden*, and *id'n*. The /s/ might also be dropped, resulting in such forms as *in't*, *inna*, and *inno*. It's a short step from here to present-day *in't it* and *innit* (Chapter 18).

Similarly, the forms based on *be* can all be negated, and are often shown thus in dialect writing, especially since the eighteenth century. *Baint* and *bain't* are probably the commonest forms, but there are many variants, such as *beant*, *bent*, *bisn't*, and *binna*. And, as with the 1st person, there's widespread use of *ain't*, with its many variants such as *en't*, *eant*, and *aren't*. Charles Dickens' characters are regular *ain't*-users: *there ain't any thing the matter; she ain't half bad*. And it even gets into modern standard English, in jocular usage and through song:

If it ain't broke, don't fix it.

'T ain't what you say, it's the way that you say it.

It ain't necessarily so...

There is no mistake; there has been no mistake; and there shall be no mistake.

Arthur Wellesley, 1st Duke of Wellington (1769–1852)
Letter to Mr Huskisson, who had written to the duke
saying there must have been some mistake in being
asked for his resignation

It depends on what the meaning of the word 'is' is. If the—if he—if 'is' means is and never has been, that is not—that is one thing. If it means there is none, that was a completely true statement. Now, if someone had asked me on that day, are you having any kind of sexual relations with Ms Lewinsky, that is, asked me a question in the present tense, I would have said no. And it would have been completely true.

Bill Clinton (1946–), giving testimony before a Grand Jury
(1998)

The isness of things is well worth studying; but it is their whyness that makes life worth living.

William Beebe (1877–1962)
from Konrad Lorenz, *On Aggression* (1963), Chapter 2

At every instant every transience is eternally that
transience. What it signifies is its own being, and
that being (as one sees so clearly when one's in
love) is the same as Being with the biggest
possible B. Why do you love the woman you're in
love with? Because she *is*. And that, after all, is
God's own definition of Himself: I am that I am.
The girl is who she is. Some of her isness spills
over and impregnates the entire universe.

Aldous Huxley (1894–1963)
The Genius and the Goddess (1955), p. 46

I was born ... with ready-made parents and a
sister and brother who had already begun their
store of experience, inaccessible to me except
through their language and the record, always
slightly different, of our mother and father, and
as each member of the family was born, each,
in a sense with memories on loan, began to
supply the individual furnishings of each
Was-land, each Is-land, and the hopes and
dreams of the Future.

Janet Frame (1924–2004)
To the Is-land (1982), Chapter 1

10

I might be being obsessive, but...

progressive *be*

For all learners of English as a foreign language, one of the earliest encounters is the use of *be* to help form the present tense: *I walk > I am walking*. The construction is variously described as the *progressive* or the *continuous*, both terms suggesting the way this form conveys a sense of duration for an action. It's often accompanied by words that reinforce the notion of time passing:

Where's John?—He's walking in the park.

It's wrong to use the simple present tense here, as is so often heard in the early stages of learning English:

Where's John?—He walks in the park.

A progressive construction with *be* is found in Old English, and develops a wide range of uses, including some that no longer exist today. In 1653 we read in a history text of 'The Romans being preparing their dinners' and in 1745 of a monarch 'being walking in the Mall'. Jane Austen writes in *Persuasion* (1818) of 'the concert being just opening'. It's a construction that lasted as long as the early twentieth century:

> Another thing about him that was not natural was his being always looking in the glass.   (Edith Nesbit, *London Magazine*, 1903)

It still has some dialect use.

Another disappeared usage is the use of the progressive with passive meaning, as in this example from some translations of the Bible: 'the ark was building', where the meaning is 'the ark was being built'. This too is recorded into the beginning of the twentieth century, but never with the frequency with which it was used in earlier centuries:

> 1530: He ordeynid that men shuld stand while the gospell was reding.
> 1784: Whilst the Anthem was singing I was conducted by the Virger to the Pulpit…
> 1859: Sir John had volunteered for the expedition which is preparing.

There's a nice double instance in Laurence Sterne's *The Life and Opinions of Tristram Shandy, Gentleman* (1761):

> At the very time that this dispute was maintaining by the centinel and the drummer—was the same point debating betwixt a trumpeter and a trumpeter's wife.

It's interesting today to note that, when the modern construction began to be used, it received severe criticism from the purists of the time. David Booth, for example, in *An Analytical Dictionary of the English Language* (1830), comments:

> For some time past, 'the bridge is *being built*,' 'the tunnel is *being excavated*,' and other expressions of a like kind, have pained the eye and stunned the ear.

And he worries lest:

> Instead of 'The stone is falling,' and 'The man is dying,' we shall next be
> taught to say, The stone is *being fallen*,' and 'The man is *being dead*.'

His observation, of course, shows that he hasn't understood the difference between transitive verbs (which take an object, as in *build a bridge* and *excavate a tunnel*), intransitive verbs (which don't, as in *the stone is falling*), and complements (like *dead* in *the man is dead*).

The progressive aspect has traditionally been used with verbs that express a dynamic action, such as *run*, *kick*, and *eat*. It would not usually be used with verbs expressing a static event, such as *see*, *know*, and *have* (*stative* verbs). Usages such as 'I'm having a cold' or 'I'm seeing a dog' would traditionally be corrected by an English teacher. But times are changing—and have been for some time. A verb with a normally static meaning can be galvanized into dynamic action if the context justifies it: 'I'm having a meeting with John next Tuesday'. There are signs of this from at least the early nineteenth century, as in this *OED* citation from 1839:

> Some were having dinner in the perambulating taverns.   (*Literary World*)

And during the twentieth century we see a gradual increase in the use of progressive *be*:

> 1920:…they had been on the ranch about a month, and were liking it
> more and more every day.
> 1963:…the rapidly succeeding series of scenes we are seeing.

Increasingly we hear it used to reduce the level of commitment, as in *I was wondering if*…and *I was just wanting to say*…A generation or so ago, people would more likely have said *I wondered if*…and *I just wanted to say*…The most famous contemporary example must be the

McDonald's slogan: 'I'm lovin' it'. That would probably have been 'I love it' back in the 1960s.

In some varieties of English, such as those used in India and Ireland, the progressive has long been used with static verbs. Usages like 'I'm knowing the answer to your question' and 'You are realizing the importance' are frequently heard, and form one of their distinctive grammatical features. Here's a threefold Irish example, from Patricia Rice's *The English Heiress* (2012):

> 'Faith, and I'm after thinking you're needing that caning your faither never gave ye,' he mocked. 'And I'm knowing just the man to do it.'

These days, we're likely to encounter the progressive used somewhere or other with any verb—but does that include *be* itself? Could *be* have a dynamic sense? There are examples that date from the seventeenth century, the earliest from Samuel Pepys' *Diary* in 1665:

> And Lord, to see how ridiculous a conceited pædagogue is, though a learned man—he is being so dogmaticall in all he doth and says.

The sense is of a property (here, dogmatism) being in evidence at a specific time and for a limited duration. There's often a contrast with a habitual or universal meaning. When Keats writes to John Hamilton Reynolds in 1819 'You will be glad to hear under my own hand…how diligent I have been, and am being', he is referring to the progress he is making with his current writing projects. And this limited temporality is evident in such situations as these:

> Stop being obnoxious.
> John is being very nice to Mary this evening.
> I'm being a real help, aren't I.
> I might be being stupid, but…

And that opens the door to the more cumbersome passive construction:

So you think your child may be being bullied.

Dozens may be being held hostage.

The plans have been being delayed for months.

Awkward they may be, especially the last one, but sometimes there isn't an easier way to say what needs to be said, especially in cases like these, where it isn't possible to identify with certainty who the perpetrators are. Who are the bullies? the hostage-takers? the delayers? We do not know—or someone is not saying. That's the function of the passive: to allow us to say that something happens without having to say who did it.

11

My kids are all grown up
perfective be

On 8 November 1808, philosopher and social reformer Jeremy Bentham writes a jocular response to a gloomy letter he's received from his cousin Mulford:

> There is a report about town, though I have not yet seen it, in the newspapers, of your being about to commit matrimony. If you do, you must not think of having my consent; for what if you should happen to tip the perch before all the children are grown up?

He does not write 'have grown up'. Why not?

The *has/have* construction forms what grammarians today call the 'perfect aspect' (or earlier, the 'perfect tense'). Its chief function is to express current relevance. If I say 'I've sprained my ankle', I want to convey that this has recently happened. The contrast is with the past tense: if I say 'I sprained my ankle', the event is pushed further back into the past.

By using *be*, the event is pulled into the present. If I say 'My kids are all grown up', I'm thinking of their present state—how they are at the time of speaking. I'm not focusing on the period of time that enabled them to reach this state. The implications are different.

Our guests have all gone—a simple statement of fact.

Our guests are all gone—finally! Now we can start to clear up.

It isn't a large semantic contrast, but it's one that writers often use, especially when they are in a nostalgic mood. Here's James R. Smith in *San Francisco's Lost Landmarks* (2005):

The shelly-cocoa and the golden and purple lupine blossoms are gone forever from all the old hillsides...

The writer wants to make us feel the loss is ours as we read.

This use of *be* can be traced back to Old English, as in this example from the *Anglo-Saxon (Parker) Chronicle* for the year 893:

Wæs Hæsten þa þær cumen mid his herge.

'literally: Was Hæsten then there come with his host.

'Then Hæsten came there with his host.'

It's found only with intransitive verbs, and mainly (especially in later centuries) with verbs of motion, such as *come, go, rise, set, arrive*, and *depart*:

These are the parents of these children, / Which accidentally are met together.   (William Shakespeare, *The Comedy of Errors*, 1594)

Satan arrives to address his followers: Therefore I am return'd.
(John Milton, *Paradise Regained*, 1671)

A good example of the potential semantic force behind the *be* usage is found in one of the acclamations used in the Roman Catholic liturgy of the Mass:

Christ has died, Christ is risen, Christ will come again.

It would of course have been possible for the liturgists to have proposed 'Christ has risen'; but the use of the present-tense form has theological significance: for believers, the resurrection of Christ is an event that actively informs their lives today. The choice also has rhetorical force, bringing together past, present, and future.

These examples are all from standard English. In regional dialects, the use of *be* has widened to take in transitive verbs as well. Examples have been collected from many parts of the English-speaking world, such as the north of Scotland (Orkney and Shetland), the Midlands of England, and the southern USA. Liturgical scholar Christopher Wordsworth observed instances of *is* replacing *has* in *Rutland Words* (1891), such as 'I am been wonderful bad'. The recorded instances in the *OED* date only from the early nineteenth century, but the usage doubtless has a much longer history. And, judging by the citations, it is still quite common today:

> 'If you kin git any mo' refreshment off a fish bone than me, you must be got two necks and a gang of bellies,' said Larkins.   (Zora Neale Hurston, *Mules and Men*, 1935)
> I is just had a stunnin' and sweepin' thought.   (Toronto *Globe & Mail*, 1968)

It turns up in some unexpected places. In each episode of the BBC comedy TV series *The Fast Show* (mid-1990s), the country bumpkin Jesse (played by Mark Williams) reports his unusual diets and fashions, saying such things as 'This week I are been mostly eatin' / wearing...'. The expression caught on. Several blogs are now headed 'This week I are been mostly...'.

Teacher. (referring to sentence on blackboard). "JOHNNIE, WHAT MUST I DO TO CORRECT THAT?"

Johnny. "TELL YOUR YOUNG MAN."

12

Wannabes and has-beens
nominal *be*

Wannabes—or, with a spelling that better suggests the pronunciation, *wannabees*—feels very much like a modern coinage. The elided pronunciation of *want to* (as in *I wanna go*) has been around for quite a while, along with *gonna* (*going to*) and *gotta* (*got to*). Instances have been recorded since the late nineteenth century, becoming increasingly common as novelists attempted to capture the natural character of colloquial speech. But it wasn't until the 1980s that somebody in the USA first used it with *be* to form a noun—a 'nominal' use—meaning (as the *OED* definition sedately puts it) 'an admirer or fan who seeks to emulate a particular celebrity or type, esp. in matters of appearance or dress'.

People who dressed like popstar Madonna formed one of the earliest trends, to the extent that a new blend emerged: *Madonna wannabes* became *Madonnabes*. The Beatles received the same kind of neologistic accolade: a tribute band called themselves *The Wannabeatles*. The Spice Girls seemed to bring the usage to a peak with their hit song *Wannabe* in 1996, but the word continues to be popular. A 2015 movie was called *The Wannabe*. And, the ultimate mark of success for a new word, it has been borrowed by other languages. A French web series is called *Les Wannabes*. A German sitcom is called *Die Wannabes*. A beauty and lifestyle periodical published in Belgrade (in Serbian) is called *Wannabe Magazine*.

The colloquial pronunciation may be recent, but the notion the word represents certainly isn't. In the form *would-be*, with the adjectival meaning of 'wishing to be' or 'intended to be', it can be traced back to the fourteenth century—'a would-be assassin', 'a would-be rustic gate'. Noun uses are found from the seventeenth century. We encounter one first in Ben Jonson's *Volpone* (1605), as a person's name: 'Sir Politique Would-bee, a Knight'. Later that century, we see it as a common noun: in Andrew Marvell's *The Rehearsal Transpros'd* (1672) some clergy are described as 'Politick would-be's'.

There's something about *be* that attracts compound usages as nouns and adjectives. Alongside *being*, as the fundamental notion that has attracted philosophers since Plato, and *beings*, especially attractive to sci-fi writers, we find many derived forms and compound expressions, such as *beingness*, *unbeing*, *well-being*, *human being*, *house of being*. The *OED* also shows a rare adjectival use of *being*, as seen in John Lydgate's 'The beeyng woord of hym that is hyhest' (mid-fifteenth century), and an even rarer comparative form in a recent theological text:

> What is counted as nothing…is said to be 'beinger' (*seiender*) or more beingful than any being.   (John Macquarrie, *In Search of Deity*)

Beingful has an adjectival antonym in *beingless*. 'Beingless beings', writes James Joyce in *Ulysses* (see p. 135 for this and other nounal examples in literature).

When it comes to *be*-compounds using auxiliary verbs, the *OED* lists several variants:

How slender these Hopes…which these *it may be's* do afford…   (from seventeenth-century clergyman Thomas Goodwin)
List, then, old Is-Was-and-To-Be!   (from nineteenth-century playwright George Colman)
[Channel 5] will be a channel for the going-to-be's, not the has-beens…
(from the twentieth-century *Daily Telegraph*)

Has-beens has come to be used in a remarkable variety of ways. It seems to have begun life in Scotland in the seventeenth century, referring to former or ancient customs: 'Gude auld has-beens'. Then it developed a more general sense of 'past event': something that happened would be described as *a has-been*. In the plural, it could mean 'old times': one might meet up with someone *for has-beens*—for old times' sake. At the same time, it came to be applied to people: anyone whose best days are over, especially someone who once was famous and is no longer so, and this is the commonest modern sense. A rather sad web story was headed: 'How to date a has-been celeb'. And the *Daily Telegraph* in 2014 reported another sad case of someone who 'moved from being a promising newcomer to a clapped-out old has-been'.

It's a noun that has developed a range of contrasts that act almost like verb tenses, as illustrated by a citation from *Tait's Edinburgh Magazine* in 1834 which brought together 'the has-been, being, and to-be'. The *Christian Parlor Magazine* in 1852 talks about 'dilapidated "has-beens", and despised "used-to-be's"'. A 2005 source links 'the has-been and the not-yet'. And one sentence has achieved semi-proverbial status: 'It's better to be a has-been than a never-was'.

Or, presumably, a 'might-have-been': a case of unfulfilled potential, or an event that might have happened. The usage seems to have developed in the nineteenth century, first as an adjective, then a noun.

Thomas Hardy uses it in *A Pair of Blue Eyes* (1873). Harry Knight tells his fearful Elfride: 'let us confine our attention to ourselves, not go thinking of might-have-beens'. Historian A. L. Rowse dismisses them, in his *Expansion of Elizabethan England* (1955): 'The might-have-beens of history are not a very profitable subject'. But J. M. Barrie has a soft spot for them, in *Dear Brutus* (1917): Margaret asks Mr Dearth, 'Daddy, what is a might-have-been?' And he replies:

A might-have-been? They are ghosts, Margaret. I dare say I 'might have been' a great swell of a painter, instead of just this uncommonly happy nobody. Or again, I might have been a worthless idle waster of a fellow.... And there are other 'might-have-beens'—lovely ones, but intangible. Shades, Margaret, made of sad folk's thoughts.

And the act ends with Margaret disappearing into a wood with the words 'I don't want to be a might-have-been'.

Most of the compound *be*-nouns relate to the past; but the future isn't excluded. Once again the adjectival usage of *to be* precedes the noun, in its sense of 'that is yet to be', with citations from the seventeenth century. Kinship terms especially attracted it: *mother-to-be, grandfather-to-be, wife-to-be*. The noun use doesn't appear until the nineteenth century, with Byron's *Ode on Venice* (1819):

The flow and ebb of each recurring age,
The everlasting to be which hath been...

That combination of future and past proved to be popular. Novelist Marie Corelli uses it in *The Master-Christian* (1900): the young reformer Cyrillon Vergniaud affirms 'I work and write for the To-Be, not the Has-Been'.

Even a combination of pronoun and verb form has been nominalized, thanks to biblical influence—the verb use in 'I am that I am' (see p. 38) of Exodus 3.14 immediately generated a noun: 'I am hath sent me unto you'. Many writers continued the usage, referring to God viewed as self-existent as 'the great I am'. But it was not long before the expression went well beyond the divine, coming to be used for any self-important person. In Sylvia Townsend Warner's novel *Lolly Willowes* (1926), we read: 'Jim thought himself quite a Great I AM'. Or other-important person: in *Lady Chatterley's Lover* (1928), D. H. Lawrence has Clifford telling Connie 'I am a cypher. You are the great I-am! as far as life goes'. Sensing her antagonism, he goes on to gloss it:

> You know that, don't you? I mean, as far as I am concerned. I mean, but for you, I am absolutely nothing. I live for your sake and your future. I am nothing to myself.

That's as full a gloss of a nominal form of *be* as we're ever likely to see.

1st, 2nd, 3rd person plural, present tense, indicative mood: we/you/they are

IN Old English, three forms competed for the role of a plural present tense of *be*. One set clustered around a form usually shown as *sind* in the grammars (as in modern German), which had such variants as *sindan*, *synden*, and *sint*. These lasted into the early Middle English period: the latest citation in the *OED* is for 1300. But by then, the other two forms had become dominant: one developed into modern *are*; the other into modern *be*.

We see the *are* set starting out in Old English in such dialect forms as *earon* and *earan* (showing an inflectional ending) and developing in Middle English as *aren, aryn, eryn, eren*, and many other variants, until the *-n* is lost, and we get such forms as *arre, er*, and the first instances of *are*. Later variants hint at regional pronunciations, such as *er* in Northern Ireland, *air* in the southern USA, and *a* in the Caribbean islands. A Kentucky source in 1974: *Air they fur hit or air they agin hit?* A Yorkshire source in 1976: *Mi senses ahr dazed.* The *are* form gradually established itself in the London area during the sixteenth century, probably the result of immigration into the capital of large numbers of *are*-speakers from the Midlands and East Anglia, and thus became the standard form.

The *be* set starts out also with dialect forms and inflectional endings, such as *beoðan* and *biðon*, then without the ending (such as *beoð* and *bieð*). During the Middle English period, we see some scribes writing the final *th* sound with a *z*, as in *beoz* and *bez*. The modern vowel sound is clearly reflected at that time in such spellings as *beet* and *beeth* and without the final consonant in *bee* and *bey*. Forms ending in *-n* are also seen in Middle English (*beon, byn, bin, bene...*), and these continued in regional dialects along with forms ending in *-s* (*be's, bees, beis...* and—recorded in Worcestershire—*bist*). Archaisms abound in historical literature:

'there be monsters', and—often on the edges of old maps, showing unknown territory—'here be dragons'. We still say *the powers that be*.

Readers of older literature have to be careful when they see *been*-forms, to avoid confusing them with a past tense. When we see Gower in Shakespeare's *Pericles* talking about the seas, 'Where when men been, there's seldome ease', he means 'are' not 'have been'. They also need to be aware that the *be*-form can express a habitual meaning, as in other persons of the verb: *they be sayin'* means 'they habitually say'.

As might be expected, after seeing the way the singular present-tense forms of *be* operate (Panels on p. 32, p. 49, and p. 60), any of the forms that are singular today are found as plurals in earlier periods. 'Ill deeds is doubled with an evil word', says Luciana in Shakespeare's *The Comedy of Errors*. Modern regional dialects use all possible forms in the plural. We see *is*-variants, especially in the north of England and Scotland. *Am*-variants are typical of African-American dialects: 'There am lots of folks...' is recorded in a 1945 source.

Contracted forms operate similarly to those in the singular. Alongside the standard colloquial *we're*, *you're*, and *they're* we find *w'are*, *y'are*, *th'are*; *we'm*, *you'm*, *they'm*; and *we's*, *you's*, *they's*. Negative forms appear likewise: alongside *aren't* we find *nare* and its variants in Old and Middle English. Later we see the same range of regional variations that occur in the 2nd person singular (Panel on p. 49):

-*are*-types: arna, yent, an't, ain't...

-*be*-types: beant, baint, binna, byunt...

-*is*-types: isn't, inna, in't...

'Y'know bor, them ole taales in't often wrong', writes John Kett in his Norfolk dialect anthology, *Tha's a Rum'un, Bor* (1973 = 'You're an odd fellow, boy'). Very true.

Conjuror. (to Harry, who has kindly stepped up to assist with the card tricks) "Now, Sir, you know what a pack of cards is?"
Harry. (determined not to be made a fool of). "I know what a pack of cards *are*!"

We are the music makers,
And we are the dreamers of dreams,
Wandering by lone sea-breakers,
And sitting by desolate streams;
World-losers and world-forsakers,
On whom the pale moon gleams:
Yet we are the movers and shakers
Of the world for ever, it seems.

Arthur O'Shaughnessy (1844–81)
'Ode' (1873)

[OPHELIA]

Lord, we know what we are, but not what
we may be.

William Shakespeare (1564–1616)
Hamlet, 4.5.42

RIDER

... we can be but
What we are.

VENTURE

A pair of credulous fools.

James Shirley (1596–1666)
Hyde Park (1632), 1.1

Sint ut sunt aut non sint.
Let them be as they are or not be at all.

Pope Clement XIII (1693–1769)
replying to a request for changes in the constitutions
of the Jesuits

Oh! what a monster-wit must that man have
That cou'd please all which now their twelve-
pence gave!
High characters (cries one) and he would see
Things that ne'er were, nor are, nor e'er will be.

John Suckling (1609–41)
The Goblins, Epilogue, l.5

How long
Is a song?
O Lord,
How long?
As long as Loew,
And Keith
And Albee:
It Was,
And Is,
And Always Shall Be.
This is the string Time may not sever.
This is the music that lasts forever.

Ogden Nash (1902–71)
'The screen with the face with the voice' (in *Good
Intentions*, 1942)

13

That is to say
signifying *be*

Be has a widely used function introducing an explanation of what has just been said. The usage is attested since the fourteenth century. One of the earliest known English wills, from 1395, includes this bequest:

I bequethe to the same Thomas, the stoffe longyng therto, that is to seye, my beste fetherbed...

and the will then lists all that is involved in 'the stuff belonging thereto'. *That is to wit* and *that is to witting* were also used in this way until the sixteenth century, when that use of *wit* (meaning 'know', 'be aware of') died out, other than in legal English *to wit*. In the twentieth century we see an increase in *which is to say*—a consequence of the uncertainty surrounding the use of *that* versus *which* caused by the strictures of nineteenth-century prescriptive grammars—but the form with *that* remains the usual one.

Outside of the law, the short form *that is* became the norm, but used in two ways. Its normal placement is deep within a clause, where it explains or amplifies what has just preceded. In Shakespeare's *Cymbeline*, Cloten tries to persuade Pisanio to do his bidding:

> undergo those employments wherein I should have cause to use thee with a serious industry, that is, what villainy soe'er I bid thee do, to perform it, directly and truly.

But the expression can also occur at the end of a clause, and here it plays a somewhat different role, expressing some kind of limitation or condition on what has just been said:

> I bet the Scotsboro' boys will be electrocuted in the end, if they don't die of old age first, that is.   (Nancy Mitford, *The Pursuit of Love*, 1945)

> 'I think finally, I shall go into the Navy.' 'You!' Nodding, still looking out of the window: 'If they'd have me, that is.'   (William Golding, *Pincher Martin*, 1956)

It seems to be a usage that caught on in the twentieth century, though there are hints of it earlier:

> Those who 'intrude' (thrust, that is) themselves into the fold.   (John Ruskin, *Sesame and Lilies*, 1865)

In the within-clause examples, someone is asserting that there is an equivalence of meaning between two expressions. We might replace the *is* by *means* or *amounts to*, and this function can be seen in a wide variety of situations where a form of the verb *be* is used without a preceding *that*. In the King James Bible (Genesis 41.26), Joseph interprets the dream of Pharaoh about seven cattle and seven ears of corn:

> The seven good kine are [= mean] seven years; and the seven good ears are [= mean] seven years...

Such usages are less definite than *that is*. In a medical textbook (1949), we read: 'To delay a few hours is to await inevitable local death'. The writer is stating a personal view, a likely outcome. It contrasts with *that is*, which is more assertive and definite. Compare:

> Happiness is a cold beer on a hot day.
> Happiness, that is, a cold beer on a hot day.

We see the personal element coming to the fore when a form of *be* is used in questions and in negative contexts, where the usage suggests an issue of particular importance or significance to a person. Typically it's followed by a phrase containing a pronoun, identifying who the person is:

> What's that to you?
> Is that nothing to him?

The narrator in George Borrow's *Lavengro* (1900) provides four examples in quick succession:

> She says she is nothing to me, even as I am nothing to her. I am of course nothing to her, but she is mistaken in thinking she is nothing to me.

The underlying sense is sometimes brought to the surface in a sequence like this: 'It may not be much to you, but it means a lot to me'. In the first episode of the British television comedy series *Only Fools and Horses* (1981), Rodney looks out of the window at their yard:

> It may not be much to you, Del, but to me it's got a raw and savage beauty.

Paradoxically, the definiteness we associate with *that is* allows it to be used in situations of a totally opposite kind, when someone is feeling uncertain or tentative, as in '…that is, if you don't mind me asking', where the sense is 'if you don't have any objection'. Mark Twain was uncharacteristically non-fluent when he met Artemus Ward for the first time, the result of unwisely drinking a whisky cocktail before the conversation began. He records what happened in 'First interview with Artemus Ward' (1871). After listening to a long and convoluted question, he stammers:

I—I—that is—if you don't mind, would you—would you say that over again?

An incapable use of *be*.

1 st and 3 rd person singular, past tense, indicative mood: I/he/she/it was

THE spelling of *was* looks as if it should be pronounced 'wass', and indeed such a pronunciation is clearly shown in the earliest recorded forms in Old English, such as *wæss* and *uæs*. The unrounded vowel and a voiceless final consonant continue to appear in Middle English (*waas, uas*…) and into the sixteenth century (*wasse, wass*…); but during that period we also see the first signs of the modern vowel in this form. The change took place because of the initial /w/, famous in the history of English for the way it alters the phonetic character of any vowel that follows. A rounded vowel is seen in such spellings as *vos, woos, wos*, and *wosse*—pronunciations that were especially found across the English

Midlands and into East Anglia, and which later spread elsewhere. Writers on 'correct' pronunciation don't start noting the rounding until the seventeenth century. The voicing of the final /s/ took place earlier, during the Middle English period, but the unvoiced form stayed until at least the 1600s. *Was* rhymes with *glass*, *grass*, and *pass* in Shakespeare, all with the 'short *a*' vowel heard in *cat*.

Judging by the regional dialect spellings, *was* has been pronounced with every possible vowel: apart from *was*, we see *wuz*, *wiz*, *wez*, and *woz*, sometimes ending in *-s* or *-ss*, and even in *-se*, *-ce*, and *-sz*. This variation carries through into the negative form. The earliest negatives in Old English, with the particle preceding the verb (*næs*, *nass*, *nes*...), died out in the sixteenth century, to be replaced by *wasn't*, and we then see this form written with all vowel letters around the regional dialects of England. There's also replacement of /z/ by /d/, as in *wadden*, *woddent*, and *wad'n*, and by /s/ in *wussin't*. The final *-t* drops in such forms as *wanna*, *wunna*, and *wasnae*. In its fullest form, *wasn't* has six phonetic units /wɒzənt/, but in colloquial speech these can reduce to three: a 1993 source records *Was a good boy, Jack, wan' I*, where the pronunciation was presumably /wɒn/.

In Middle English we see the singular form also expressed by *were*, with all the vowel spellings appearing again: *war*, *wer*, *wor*, *wur*, *wir*. In the negative, the *were*-forms are seen in such contexts as 'he weren't ready', 'I warn't troubled', 'it worrant me', and 'there wahrn't no water in the well', with the spellings again showing typical dialect variation. The two forms *was* and *were* were often interchangeable at first, following the pattern seen in other verbs, where there was no longer any distinction between singular and plural in the past tense (*I/you/he/she/it/we/they ran/saw/went...*).

Both also appeared in contracted and negative constructions: on the one hand we see *wast* and *was't* ('Where was't?'), and, with the *it* preceding, *twas* and *'twas* ('''Twas mine'); on the other hand, we see parallel usages in *twere* and *'twere*. These forms today are encountered only in historical or poetic contexts, though we do occasionally hear them in mock-archaic speech: '''Twas ever thus...'.

A heavily contracted form of *was* is recorded in some US regional dialects, especially with the 1st person plural, variously spelled *-ze*, *'se*, *-'s*, or *-'uz*. Citations are few—just one in the nineteenth century and two in the twentieth, such as this one, from 1972: 'I's studyin' about it th'other day'. Although rare, the usage is worth noting, as it's unusual to see a present-tense form simultaneously changing number and tense. Also uncommon is the use of *am* to mean 'was', mainly in US dialects, as in this 1969 example from New Jersey: 'Alfalfa didn't come to our country when I'm a boy'.

Creole varieties of English around the world show the use of *be* to mean 'was', as in this 1953 example noted in the journal *American Speech*: 'We was all listenin' to de preachuh...Evuhbody wonder what de trouble be'. And in

94

Ireland, there are instances recorded of a past-time use of *be to* and *beet to* meaning 'have to': 'I beet to sit down, for my legs couldn't hould me'. The usage thus allows an unusual double construction, as in this example from Donegal in 1953: 'He saw a light moving through the trees—it be to be a ghost'.

As time went by, the use of *were* as a singular form ('I were there': see Panel on p. 110) and of *was* as a plural form ('we wuz going') developed during the seventeenth century into one of the most noticeable features of regional speech, especially in the north of England. By the time Charles Dickens was writing, it had become a regular way of distinguishing between educated and uneducated speech. In *Pickwick Papers* (1837), we see Serjeant Buzfuz asking Mrs Cluppins what she had heard: 'Was one of those voices Pickwick's?' She replies: 'Yes, it were, Sir'. Today it remains non-standard, but it has lost its association with lack of education, being widely heard in the media in the informal speech of (perfectly well-educated) people with a regional background.

Sergeant. "As you was!"

Yound Officer. " 'As you were,' you should say."

Sergeant. " 'Scuse me, Sir, I knows my drill. 'As you was' for one man; 'as you were' for two; 'as you was' for a squad!"

[HENRY, *to Falstaff*]
    Presume not that I am the thing I was,
    For God doth know, so shall the world perceive,
    That I have turned away my former self;
    So will I those that kept me company.
    When thou dost hear I am as I have been,
    Approach me, and thou shalt be as thou wast,
    The tutor and the feeder of my riots;

William Shakespeare (1564–1616)
Henry IV Part 2, 5.5.59

          [*Of Moloc*]
          His trust was with th' Eternal to be deem'd
          Equal in strength, and rather then be less
          Cared not to be at all.

        John Milton (1608–74)
        Paradise Lost (1667), Book 2, l.46

'Twas the night before Christmas, when all
through the house
No creature was stirring, not even a mouse.

Clement Clarke Moore (1779–1863)
'A Visit from St Nicholas' (1823)

        The three blasts of the angel filled all the
        universe. Time is, time was, but time shall
        be no more.

        James Joyce (1882–1941)
        Portrait of the Artist as a Young Man (1916), Chapter 3

I wish I were what I was when I wished
I were what I am.
Graffito reported in Nigel Rees, *Graffiti Lives OK* (1979)

14

You're cheeky, you are
repetitive be

Colloquial speech often repeats a form of *be* as a way of adding emphasis or drawing special attention to something that's been said, or is about to be said. The emphatic use has been recorded since the early nineteenth century, and appears with all persons:

I'm my own woman, I am.   (Desmond Bagley, *The Snow Tiger*, 1975)

You're a deep little puss, you are.   (George Eliot, *Silas Marner*, 1861)

Our governor's wide awake, he is.   (Charles Dickens, *Sketches by Boz*, 1835)

Sometimes the subject and verb are inverted, the past tense used, and/or the pronoun replaced by a name:

He's a sad pickle is Sam!   (Mary Russell Mitford, *Our Village*, 1828)

He was an honest man, was Patrick.   (Paul Gallico, *The Steadfast Man*, 1958)

She's very sympathetic, Daphne is.   (Rose Macaulay, *Keeping up Appearances*, 1928)

In all cases, the emphasis is only possible by using the repeated *be-*form in the shortened sentence. We would never repeat the first part as a whole: 'Our governor's wide awake, he is wide awake', 'She's very sympathetic, Daphne is very sympathetic'.

Along with these examples, the *OED* cites the following sentence from Hilaire Belloc's *Wolsey* (1930), which is doing something different:

It is a rare function, is industry upon this level.

Here the semantic 'meat' is in the second part of the sentence. The first part does little more than set the scene. It's an early instance of a usage that has attracted a great deal of attention in linguistics because of its unusual use of a 'double *is*':

The thing is / is that the exam question was ambiguous.

In writing, the rhythmical break shown by the slash is often (but not always) represented by a comma.

It's quite common in informal speech, with the first element replaced by such focusing phrases as *the truth is*, *the reason is*, *the question is*, *the point is*, and sometimes more complex phrases:

The fact of the matter is is that we need to keep campaigning.

When written down like that, without a slash or comma, it looks as if the speaker has made a tiny stammer. But sentences like these are very different from what happens during a stammer. Stammering is characterized by erratic rhythm and pausing, whereas these sentences have a definite prosody: the first *is* is stressed; it's usually followed by a brief pause; and the constructions on either side of the two *is*'s are said with a unifying rhythm showing that the speaker is very much in control.

The reasons for the usage are partly psychological, partly semantic. Because such phrases as *the thing is* contain very little concrete meaning, they can be used as a way of giving speakers time to plan the important part of what they want to say, and listeners a sense of anticipation. And because what is being said is felt to be of special importance, the mid-sentence break focuses the listener's attention on the assertion in a way that would be lost if the sentence were said as a syntactic whole:

> The thing is that the exam question was ambiguous.
>
> The fact of the matter is that we need to keep campaigning.

The 'wait for it' moment has been lost. And, it can be argued, the sentences have become a little more difficult to process.

The idiomatic function of the opening, attention-drawing element has prompted its description as a 'focusing formula'; and 'double' or 'reduplicated' *is* sentences as a whole have been succinctly labelled the *2B* or *ISIS* constructions—though the latter term is probably no longer in favour, having been overtaken by world political events. They've sometimes been criticized—though not by linguists—as 'lazy', 'careless', or 'ungrammatical'. I view them as a perfectly normal feature of informal spontaneous speech. They would be avoided in formal standard English, of course, and it would be unusual to see them in writing, other than in fiction. But there are no grounds for the claim that such sentences would be used only by uneducated people or in regional dialects. Take this one:

> What has to happen is / is that the money has to come from somewhere.

That came from one of the world's most eloquent speakers during an informal debate: Barack Obama.

There's one other use of a repeated *be* that relates to the above, when someone says *I am what I am*. The speaker is saying that 'this is my true nature, my real character', is implying an unwillingness or inability to change, and is strongly suggesting that the listeners accept the situation. Any pronoun might be used: *we are what we are*, *she is what she is*, and so on. The expression is probably biblical in origin. Paul writes in 1 Corinthians 15 (in the King James Bible, 1611):

> For I am the least of the Apostles, that am not meet to be called an Apostle because I persecuted the Church of God. But by the grace of God I am what I am.

The expression caught on. Beaumont and Fletcher used it a few years later in their play *Cupid's Revenge* (1615):

> I am what I am, and they that prove me, shall find me to their cost.

And centuries later we find it still popular:

> Don't leave me, Basil, and don't quarrel with me. I am what I am. There is nothing more to be said.   (Oscar Wilde, *The Picture of Dorian Gray*, 1891)
> I'm not going around putting on no side—I am what I am, an' that's what I'm gonna be.   (Johnny Speight, *Till Death us do Part: Scripts*, 1973)

It became the name of the song that closed the first act of the Broadway musical *La Cage aux Folles* (1983). And soon after, it was a major hit when Gloria Gaynor recorded it, to the delight of the international gay pride movement: 'I am what I am / And what I am needs no excuses / I deal my own deck sometimes / The aces sometimes the deuces'.

15
Been and done it
eventive be

In Thackeray's *Vanity Fair* (1848), we learn that 'Sir Pitt has been and proposed for to marry Miss Sharp, wherein she has refused him, to the wonder of all'. We can get a sense of the function of *be* here if we contrast it with a *be*-less version:

Sir Pitt has been and proposed for to marry Miss Sharp.
Sir Pitt has proposed for to marry Miss Sharp.

The latter is a simple statement of fact. The former adds a speaker attitude. It could be delight, surprise, excitement, annoyance, anger—virtually anything, depending on the accompanying intonation and facial expression. But whatever the attitude, the *has been* gives a dynamic thrust to the verb that follows, suggesting that its action was unexpected or unusual.

It's a very restricted construction, amplifying the perfective aspect of the main verb, and only that. We can't use it with other *be*-forms. We can't say such things as 'He'll be and propose to…', or 'He's being and proposing to…', or 'He was and proposed to…'. It seems to have emerged in the eighteenth century as a way of adding emphasis in colloquial speech. Here's the first recorded use, in Francis Coventry's adventures of a lap-dog called *The History of Pompey the Little* (1752):

I'll be whipped if this *owdacious* little dog has not been and thrown down my lady's backside's breakfast.

Charles Dickens uses it often, as in *Bleak House* (1853):

One of the young Jellybys been and got his head through the area railings!

It's never gone out of use, though its popularity waned somewhat in the late nineteenth century. Here are some present-day examples:

Have you been and taken a look at our new and exciting website?

The rabbit's been and eaten my crisps.

Sports reporting produces many instances, such as when a footballer 'has been and scored'.

The waning in popularity was probably due to the rise of an even more emphatic alternative using *go*. The first recorded usage is just a little earlier than *been and*, in Abraham Langford's ballad opera *The Lover his own Rival* (1736):

'Tis well if he don't go and hang himself, to be reveng'd of us.

Go was a much more dynamic verb, and also a lot more flexible than *be*. It could be used emphatically with different tenses and numbers:

He goes and gets himself married.

Look what she's gone and done.

They'll go and get themselves killed if they carry on like that.

It was then only a matter of time before a doubly intensified construction emerged, using both verbs—to begin with, in either order. For instance, we see *go* before *be* in this example from Dickens' *The Cricket on the Hearth* (1844):

> I hope nobody an't gone and been and died if you please!

But the crescendo effect conveyed by the order BE > GO > ACTION evidently proved more attractive, as part of everyday eloquence, and this became the norm. The commonest sequence has *done* as the main verb, illustrated by the *OED*'s first citation, from W. S. Gilbert's *Bab Ballads* (1869, p. 218):

> The padre said, 'Whatever have you been and gone and done?'

Any dynamic verb could replace *done*, as in 'We've been and gone and got married' and 'I've been and gone and told him so'. But it was 'done' that appealed to writers and cartoonists.

These days, nothing to my mind identifies the colloquial success of a construction more than when it is used as the title of a pop song. The accolade was achieved in 1967 when Glasgow band Studio 6 recorded 'Bless My Soul (I've Been And Gone And Done It)'. But it was fifteen minutes of fame. In 1979, Swedish group Abba were working on a new track for their second 'greatest hits' compilation, and chose 'Been and Gone and Done It' as the title. In the end, the song came out with the title 'Gimme! Gimme! Gimme! (A Man After Midnight)'. Björn Ulvaeus explained his change of mind: 'It's an old expression that means you have got married. It was a nice idea, but in the end I thought it was a bit too old-fashioned.' Fame over.

16

Have you been?
lavatorial *be*

This expression must have started out as a shortened form of a full sentence, such as *Have you been to the lavatory?*, avoiding the potentially embarrassing 'dirty word'. Its first recorded use is quite recent, 1959. *Go* is used in a similar way (*I need to go*), and there's evidence of that from the 1920s. I suspect that this use of *be* is much older, reaching back to an era of Victorian fastidiousness. Exploring its history introduces us to a shadowy domain where words hide unpleasant realities—a world of euphemisms.

Because it's not the sort of thing one often writes about in polite society, records of earlier usage are sparse. Even the Romantic poets, with their fascination with things earthy and everyday, avoid the subject. Do we know anything about the toileting practices of William Wordsworth? We do not. But there is some evidence that these colloquial expressions are very old indeed.

How did the Anglo-Saxons say they'd 'been'? Abbot Ælfric, writing a sermon around the year 1000, tells a story about Arrius, a heretic who called a council to attack the local bishop. The bishop prayed that God would show who was right, and Ælfric tells what happened (in my translation):

> They came there in the morning to the council. Then the heretic said to his companions that he wished to go for his necessary purpose. Then he came to the privy and sat down. Then all his entrails turned out at his stool, and he sat there dead. Thus God showed that he was just as empty in his belief as he was in his intestines.

Ælfric writes: 'he to gange com'—literally, 'he to a going-place came'.

The word for 'privy' in Old English was *gang*, also spelled *gong*. It comes from the verb 'go', *gangan*—a verb we still hear in Scots English: 'Will ye gang along wi' me?' In Anglo-Saxon times there was a whole family of words based on *gang*. A privy could be called a *gang-ern* ('going-urn'), a *gang-pyt* ('going-pit'), a *gang-setl* ('going seat'), or a *gang-tun* ('going house'). One of the worst jobs in the world must have been that of an Anglo-Saxon *gang-feormere* ('privy cleaner').

One 'goes' to the toilet. More elegantly one might 'visit' it. But, having gone, we do not usually say *I've gone* or ask children if they *have gone*. We can say *I went an hour ago*, but not *I've gone an hour ago*. *Been* does the job instead. *I've been*. *Been* as a past form of *go*. Unusual.

Have you been? Parents know that this is a very important question before starting out on a long car journey with children, or engaging in some similar enterprise where the inaccessibility of a toilet is a critical factor. But it's an odd usage, for it's socially highly restricted. It's only used by adults talking to little children or to people they are treating like little children. One of the complaints adult hospital patients have is when nursing staff speak to them patronizingly in this way: 'Have you been today, David?' 'Yes, nurse.' And then David gets praised. (Or told off, if the answer is 'No.')

There's an echo of this at the end of a chapter ('Talkers') in Klare Sullivan's 2002 memoir on changing times in the American South, *A Full Cup: Living, Loving, and Laughing in the 80's*. In the last of eight scenes of 'girl talk' (presented along the lines of Jacques' 'seven ages of man' speech in Shakespeare's *As You Like It*) we read:

> Act III, Scene II. We see two ladies—most definitely over-the-hillers. They are speaking, but their words are more like a whisper. One of them is saying, 'Have you been today?'
> 'No, but I'm hoping,' and the curtain closes with that great expectation!

The usage is also restricted to the *have/had been* form of the verb. If a child says 'No', and is promptly despatched to the bathroom, the parent does not then call out *Are you being*? Nor are there such questions as *Will you be*? or *Were you being*? The only possibility is *I've been*, or a variant thereof. In William Golding's *Free Fall* (1959) we read:

> ... finally, among the singing stars, I'd been, three times, and couldn't pee any more.

And I once heard a sufferer from diarrhoea say *I've been being all morning*. It was not an existential reflection.

2nd person singular, all forms plural, past tense, indicative mood: you/we/they were

As with the present tense (Panel on p. 49), there's no longer a difference between the past tense 2nd person singular and plural: both are *were*. Their histories run along parallel lines, so it makes sense to take them together.

In Old English, the singular form was similar to what we know today, with some regional variation (*were*, *wære*, *uoere*...). Forms like these carry on into Middle English, along with forms ending in *-n* (*weren*, *wern*...). The /r/ was always pronounced, and is noticeable in such spellings as *warre*. Forms with /r/ are still the most commonly encountered today around the world, though not in Received Pronunciation, which developed as an *r*-less accent towards the end of the eighteenth century.

During the Middle English period we see attempts being made to distinguish singular *were* from plural *were*, by transferring the *-st* ending used in other verbs (as in *thou walkedst*) or the *-t* ending (*thou shalt*) to produce such forms as *werst*, *werest*, and especially *wert*. *Thou wert* thus became an intimate or informal option, contrasting with *ye weren*, later *ye were*, and then *you were*, as a polite singular form.

We can see the development in several texts of the period. In the Wycliffe translation of the Bible (*c*.1384, John 1) we read 'Whanne thou were vndir the fyge tree'. In Tyndale's translation, a generation later, we read 'When thou wast…' — a usage that continues in the King James Bible (1611). The *wert* form eventually died out of everyday English, but remained a favourite usage among poets. A well-known example occurs in Shelley's ode to the skylark in *Prometheus Unbound* (1820): 'Hail to thee, blithe spirit! Bird thou never wert'.

Once *were* was established as the standard form, we see the dialect spellings starting to appear, such as *war* and *wur*, along with their negative and contracted forms. Forms with a preceding negative particle (*nære*, *nere*…) die out by the thirteenth century. *Weren't* is established by the seventeenth century. A remarkable number of dialect forms are recorded. Some seem to be simply a non-standard spelling of the pronunciation, such as *wurnt*, but most involve a change of some kind, as seen in *warna*, *warn't*, and *werna*, the distinctive *wurden* and *wurdent*, and the forms that retain the *-st* or *-t* of earlier times (*wursn't*, *wurstn't*, *wertn't*)—sometimes both together, as in *wertstn't* (recorded in Wiltshire), *wertst-na* (in Staffordshire), and *weredestn't* (in Somerset). Regional forms without the /r/ appear in *want*, *waun't*, *wunna*, and *wanna* (this last not to be confused with the colloquial pronunciation of *want to*).

Just as *were* came to be used as a singular alternative to *was* (Panel on p. 92), so *was* came to be used as a plural alternative to *were*, first with *thou* or *thee*, later with *ye* or *you*. So we find 'þu wass unnderr an fic-tre' ('You were under a fig-tree') in the twelfth-century *Ormulum*, and later forms such as *thou wast*, along with several dialect variants (*wass, wez, wiz, wust*…). The negative forms go in all directions. Some relate to *wast* and *wert*, as in *wastn't*, *wustna*, and *wuz'nst*; others relate to *was*, as in *wasn't*, *wasna*, and *wuzzent*.

Thou was is still found at later times, as in Robert Burns' *Tam o' Shanter* (1790): 'She tauld thee weel thou was a skellum' [= waster]. But *you was* becomes the norm, initially without any hint of 'incorrectness': Horace Walpole, in a letter to Richard West in 1735, reminds him of the time 'when you was at Eton'. But after the prescriptive grammarians got hold of it, it became consigned to the category of non-standard English, where it remains to this day, being allowed out only for special occasions, such as for the duet between Dean Martin and Peggy Lee, 'You Was'.

The plural uses of *were* show exactly the same kinds of historical development as the singular, except that they would never be used with *thee* or *thou*. With three persons to cope with (*we, you, they*) there are far more variants recorded—the *OED* lists 143, from Old English *uuærun* and *wære* to present-day *war* and *wur*. A few distinctive dialect contracted forms appear in the nineteenth century, such as *'rn*: 'It wur his birthday', writes a Lancashire folklorist in 1901, 'so they'rn havin' a bit ov a stir'. Similarly, the plural use of *was*, recorded continuously from the 1400s, gradually acquires a non-standard status, in the same way as *were* did for the singular.

Today we're likely to encounter plural *was* only in jocular use, but some instances are popular—as when a newspaper report of a lost football game reports a depressed fan's comment: 'we wuz robbed'. The expression has become a catchphrase for any sporting defeat considered to be unfair or undeserved. It even became a book title: *We Was Robbed: Yet More Football Poems* (1997). And, as is the way with catchphrase idioms, it has had a new literal lease of life. It's quite routine nowadays to see it heading a report of a theft or burglary. And not long ago I heard an elegant gentleman leaving a London store sympathetically complaining to a companion about the cost of a purchase with the words 'You was robbed'. The accent was Received Pronunciation. It didn't quite work, somehow.

To me, fair friend, you never can be old,
For as you were when first your eye I eyed,
Such seems your beauty still.

William Shakespeare (1564–1616)
Sonnet 104, opening lines

> Bliss in possession will not last;
> Remember'd joys are never past;
> At once the fountain, stream, and sea,
> They were—they are—they yet shall be.
>
> James F. Montgomery (1771–1854)
> 'The Little Cloud', final lines

We were at sea now, for a very long voyage—we
were to pass through the entire length of the
Levant; through the entire length of the
Mediterranean proper, also, and then cross the
full width of the Atlantic—a voyage of several
weeks. We naturally settled down into a very
slow, stay-at-home manner of life, and resolved
to be quiet, exemplary people, and roam no more
for twenty or thirty days. No more, at least, than
from stem to stern of the ship. It was a very
comfortable prospect, though, for we were tired
and needed a long rest. We were all lazy and
satisfied, now, as the meager entries in my
note-book (that sure index, to me, of my
condition), prove.

Mark Twain (1835–1910)
The Innocents Abroad (1869), Chapter 59

BENEDICK

They swore that you were almost sick for me.

BEATRICE

They swore that you were well-nigh dead for me.

William Shakespeare (1564–1616)
Much Ado about Nothing, 5.4.80

Joyce Grenfell reports a story of an American mother who wanted her daughter to learn by heart Shelley's 'Ode to a Skylark'. Her editor comments: 'There can be no more delicious moment in modern light entertainment than that in which this exponent of American culture says, "No dear, I don't know what it was if bird it never wert".'

James Roose-Evans (ed.), *Darling Ma: Letters to her Mother, 1932–44* (letters of Joyce Grenfell, 1988)
letter of 5 January 1941

17
So be it
factual *be*

So be it seems to be the last surviving member of a cluster of expressions that arose in Middle English, each acting as a kind of complex conjunction, and each conveying the notion of something 'being the case' or 'being a fact':

> *be so*: Be so þat he wille kisse me, / Euer eft we schul frendes be.
> (*Guy of Warwick, c.*1330)
> *be it*: And be it indeed that I haue erred.   (King James Bible, 1611, Job 19)
> *if so were*: If so were that the quene were brought on that morn to the
> fyre, shortely they all wolde rescow her.   (Thomas Malory, *Morte Darthur, c.*1470)

Other variants were *it so being, be it so, so be,* and *so be it.* In each instance we could replace the words with an expression such as 'suppose (that)' or 'if it were the case (that)'.

Eventually *sobeit* came to be used as a single word, and developed the sense of 'provided that' or 'if only'. The political historian Nathaniel Bacon writes in 1647:

They might have any thing sobeit they would suffer him to enjoy his Crown.

In some circles, it was a permitted alternative to *Amen* at the end of a prayer. In Wycliffe's translation of the Bible (1382), the Lord's Prayer in St Matthew's Gospel (Chapter 6) ends with the words: 'Amen, *that is so be it*'.

Howbeit too developed as a single word, with the sense of 'though' or 'although'. In Shakespeare's *Othello*, Iago reflects on Othello's character:

The Moor—howbeit that I endure him not—
Is of a constant, loving, noble nature.

Neither usage seems to have outlived the seventeenth century. *If so be* lasted longer, at least until the mid-1800s. An issue of the *Cornhill Magazine* in 1861 has the example:

It's my opinion that any man can be a duke if so be it's born to him.

Today we would say simply 'if'.

Albeit is the only conjunction of this kind to have survived to the present day, with the same sense as *howbeit*. It can be followed by a clause (sometimes along with *that*):

…albeit we have to be ready to handle the situation.
…albeit that many of the requirements are difficult to meet.

But the commonest use today is to have it followed by a single word or phrase:

The problem can be solved, albeit with some difficulty.

It is now a single unit (never written *all be it*), so we also find it used after a plural:

> The problems can be solved, albeit with some difficulty.

The clausal uses are increasingly being restricted to very formal styles, and are infrequent even there, but the phrasal use is often seen, as in this headline from *The Independent* in 2015:

> How to age successfully…albeit a little disgracefully.

The phrasal use seems to be on the increase these days, especially in the USA. Perhaps this is because people are remembering its etymology, and finding that the more emphatic meaning—'although it is true (that)'—better expresses what they want to say than the simple *although*.

The notion of something 'being the case' has also resulted in another conjunctional use of *be*: *being*, either on its own, or followed by *that* or *as*. The usage arose in the sixteenth century—Thomas More writes in one of his dialogues: 'Beyng thogh they wer but men'. We would today say *seeing that* or *since*. Followed by *that* we find examples like this one, in a Jane Austen letter in 1813:

> I am tired of Lives of Nelson, being that I never read any.

The usage was becoming increasingly colloquial, and eventually it ended up as non-standard, though often heard regionally, especially when followed by *as*. George Eliot is the first recorded user:

> '…why didna ye come to live in this country, bein' as Mrs. Poyser's your aunt too?'   (Lisbeth Bede, in *Adam Bede*, 1859)

In the nineteenth century, *being* as a conjunction is also recorded with the sense of 'if':

> 'I would take it kind, Miss, if you'd read me that story yourself, being you're not too weary.'   (Francis Hindes Groome, *Kriegspiel: The War Game*, 1896)

There are no later citations, though I imagine the usage lives on in some regional dialects.

Who uses *so be it* today? It turns out to be remarkably common as an expression of resignation ('there's nothing else we can do') or reluctant acceptance. The archaic ring to the word order makes it appeal to a wide constituency. It's been used several times to headline an article about a historical event, especially if it has a legal or religious theme. It was the title of a 2014 film documentary on the role of Buddhism in Thai society. Moving in very different directions, it has been used as the name of a film company in Texas, a card game in a series based on *Star Wars*, and a soft-porn magazine. And it turns up in pop songs: it was the title of an album by Scottish rock group The Silencers in 1995, and of a new release by singer Lisa Stansfield in 2014—with the words emblazoned on an accompanying T-shirt.

It is impossible to predict where *so be it* will turn up next. What I find especially remarkable is that it can even provide content for a media headline. My favourite is one I saw in 2011:

Alan Rickman Ends Pizza Delivery Order With Ominous 'So Be It'.

18

I live in Wales, innit?
declarative be

Innit is news. In 2008, a London teenager called directory enquiries to book a taxi to take her to an airport, and ended up having a piece of furniture delivered. According to the newspaper reports, she said 'I want a cab, innit', and—having been put through to a retail store—in due course she was sent a cabinet. Whether it happened, or whether the story was a hoax, the word made the headlines.

As it did in 2013, when Harris Academy in London banned slang words from the classroom. Several words were involved, but the headline in the *Guardian* report chose this one:

Banning slang will only further alienate young people, innit.

It's the 'go to' word for anyone writing about modern 'yoofspeak'. Martin Baum called his Shakespeare parodic translation *To Be or Not To Be, Innit* (2008). Iain Aitch's irreverent take on what it means to be British was called *We're British, Innit* (2010). By 2011 its popular presence had increased so much that it was added to the latest edition of the 'Scrabble Bible': *Collins Official Scrabble Words*.

Innit was also included in a guide produced by Tesco in 2007 explaining teenage slang for the benefit of any older check-out staff who might be confused by it. *That's phat, brotha! Innit?* said the *Daily Mail*. ['That's cool, mate.'] What was interesting about this, from a linguistic point of view, was the way the article glossed *innit*: 'Isn't it? Is it? You know? Oh, really?' This was actually quite perceptive. There's far more to *innit* than it being simply a colloquial pronunciation of *isn't it*.

Historically, that's how it probably began, sometime in the mid-twentieth century. In rapid informal speech, first the middle [t] of *isn't it* was dropped, then the [z]. The well-established *ain't* may have been an influence on it too. The earliest instance in written form so far discovered is in Michael Gilbert's thriller *Blood and Judgement* (1959): a young London boy, Ray, having discovered a body, asks his friends for confirmation: 'That's right, innit?' So it must have been around in speech for some time before that.

If it had stayed a colloquial form of *isn't it*, used as a tag for a statement in the present tense with an impersonal third person (*it/this/that is, isn't it?*), *innit* wouldn't have raised an eyebrow. What has fascinated everyone is the way it has come to be used as a tag for other verb forms, regardless of the person, number, and tense, and ignoring whether the statement is positive or negative. So we hear (with the standard English equivalents shown):

I'm going, innit? *instead of* aren't I?
You're not going, innit? *instead of* are you?
She's going, innit? *instead of* isn't she?
They were going, innit? *instead of* weren't they?
You didn't go, innit? *instead of* did you?

And so on. *Innit* has become what linguists call an *invariant tag question*, working in the same way as *n'est-ce pas* in French or *nicht wahr* in German—or, for that matter, like *eh* in several English dialects, such as Canadian.

What the Tesco glosses showed was that this tag has developed a much broader range of functions than those expressed by the traditional tag question of standard English. The basic functions of a tag question are to get the listener to agree with, verify, or corroborate something that has just been said, with the pitch patterns conveying attitudes that range from warmth to belligerence. But when a speaker introduces several *innits* into a narrative, often without stopping for a response, something else is going on:

> … so he gave me a pound, innit, and asked me to get change, and I went into that shop by your house, innit, and …

Here the tag seems to be acting as a conversational filler, like *you know* or *you see*—expressions that keep the flow of a story going, and build rapport between speaker and listener. The speaker is basically saying, in such phrases, 'you know what I'm talking about'. Sociologists would say that they're helping to build solidarity.

These next examples show a further function:

> … it was a really fantastic show, innit!
> … that was years ago, innit!

The exclamation mark conveys that the *innit* was said with a falling pitch pattern, making it sound like an exclamatory statement rather than a question. The effect is to emphasize the point. The meaning conveyed is something like 'I'm telling you' or 'definitely'. It's drawing the listener's attention to what the speaker thinks is the most important point.

And what about this one?

Speaker A: It was a really fantastic show.
Speaker B: Innit.

Here the meaning is something like 'I agree' or 'It certainly was'.

Who's using *innit*? It was first noticed in the speech of London youngsters, like Ray in Michael Gilbert's story, but since then it's been heard in several other parts of the UK, and seems to be spreading around the regions. It is especially common in Wales, where the influence of Welsh has long motivated the use of *isn't it* as an invariant tag. And it is very widely used abroad, in the 'new Englishes' that have been developing around the world, in such places as Singapore, Nigeria, and Indonesia. In fact it's been noted in over forty English-speaking countries (though not the USA), and it may well have been immigrants from the West Indies or India (or both) who introduced it into East London.

However, invariable tags have long been a feature of the Celtic-speaking areas of Britain. The *OED* has a first recorded usage of *is it* from Ireland in 1907, in J. M. Synge's *Playboy of the Western World*:

You'll be wedding them this day, is it?

And sentences like 'You're ready to go, is it?' and 'She's a good swimmer, isn't it?' are commonplace, not only in Ireland, but in Scotland and Wales. *Is it?* is often used while repeating part of a previous utterance, to express surprise or disbelief:

Speaker A: I'd like another drink.
Speaker B: A drink, is it?

And in South Africa, as well as in some British Afro-Caribbean speech, it is used with the general meaning of 'really?', 'is that so?', 'I see', expressing attitudes ranging from polite interest to incredulity, sometimes questioning, sometimes stating:

> Speaker A: I did nothing wrong.
> Speaker B: Is it.

So although immigrants to Britain will certainly have given invariant tags a boost, they may have been there already, unrecorded in writing, and unnoticed.

Driver of antiquated Bus. "BE YOU GOING TO TIPTREE?"
Passenger. (who has waited patiently). "YES, I BE."
Driver. "WELL, I BEANT."

19

So I was, like, 'wow'
quotative *be*

'Valley Girl', by American songwriter Frank Zappa, came out in 1982, and provides the *OED* with its first recorded (sic) use of a *be*-form introducing direct speech. The lyrics, delivered as a monologue behind the music by his fourteen-year-old daughter, Moon Unit Zappa, include lines like these:

> It's like 'barf me out'.
> She's like 'Oh my God'.

The valley in question was the San Fernando Valley in California. Exactly where and when the usage actually began isn't known— presumably during the 1970s—but what *is* clear is that it quickly spread throughout the state and beyond, becoming a feature of 'Valleyspeak'— or 'Valspeak'. The speech style reached Britain soon after, thanks to American TV series and movies, and eventually became so widely recognized that it provided British comedian Catherine Tate, among others, with a rich source for parody sketches.

Although *like* has been the word that has attracted all the publicity, it's the *be*-form that gives it the force of introducing a quotation ('quotative *like*')—something that would normally be shown in writing using inverted commas. But *like* isn't the only word that performs this function. It can be replaced, as these *OED* examples show:

> At first I thought it was a cool thing to do and I'm all, 'Hey, give me a smoke.'
>
> Do you know Martin Sharp? And I was, you know, Yeah, sort of.

Or there may be no intervening words at all:

> And this guy's going, 'Hey bro, what's happenin'?' And I'm, 'Hey, give me that!'
>
> I'm walking down Washington Avenue, and I'm, why is there this crowd of people there in front?

In all cases, it's the *be*-form that's needed to introduce the speech that follows—though, as the last example shows, the speech may not actually be audible. The 'Washington Avenue' walker is thinking this, not saying it aloud.

The term 'reported speech' or 'direct speech' isn't totally accurate, therefore. Even if the words are being spoken aloud, the speaker isn't concerned to present them to the listener in any accurate way. Rather, the aim is to convey the gist of what was said. It's a paraphrase, rather than a transcription. It's also a personal interpretation of what happened: the speaker has selected the bits of the event that make the best narrative, and is giving a response or reaction to it. Many instances express strength of emotion, and are reinforced by facial expression or accompanying gesture. Indeed, the non-verbal behaviour may even replace the words, so that we encounter examples such as:

And I was just like, [making a face].

So he was all [gestures with hands to show someone drinking], you know?

It's speech as drama—and in this respect the usage shares its function with the dramatic use of the historic present tense (as in *Three weeks ago, I'm walking down the street when...*).

The dramatic function is also seen in the way the style can be used to present the speech of two or more people—in effect, a mini-dialogue. Zubaida Ula, in Moisés Kaufman's play *The Laramie Project* (2001), tells of his reactions to people who ask him about his headwear:

So I'll be like, 'Well, it's part of my religion,' and they'll be—this is the worst part cuz they'll be like, 'I know it's part of your religion, but why?'

The dramatic function is sometimes described as 'mimetic'—the speaker is trying to recreate the audiovisual character of the discourse being reported.

Examples like the non-verbal ones or the 'Washington Avenue' one are important, because they show that the quotative function of *be* is doing something that other 'verbs of speaking' don't. We can replace *be* or *be like* by *say* in examples like this one:

I'm, 'Hey, give me that!' [> I said 'Hey, give me that!']

But we can't use *said* in the following example:

And I was just like, [making a face].

The linguistic value of quotative *be* or *be like* is that it is more general in meaning than any other verb in the language (except one)—even broader than *communicate*: it can be used to introduce people speaking, thinking, imagining, gesturing, and using their faces. And it covers all modes of speaking, from muttering to screaming, as well as non-linguistic oral behaviour:

So I'm, like, 'Aaaargh!'

The exception? The quotative use of *go*, as in this *OED* quotation:

'Yo-yo-yo-yo-yoe,' went the first boy. 'Yo-yo-yo-yoe!' went the second.

This is a much older use, in fact, probably developing out of an even earlier use of *go* to express object sounds ('My heart went pit-a-pat'). The *OED* quotation is from Charles Dickens, in 1836. The citations show that the present tense use in particular ('So he goes, "Never!"') significantly increased in frequency during the twentieth century.

Is there a difference between *say*, *be*, and *go* in this context? Compare:

So I said, 'They'll never do it.'
So I was, like, 'They'll never do it.'
So John went, 'They'll never do it.'

Say is used when the language is more factual; *be* and *go* when the speaker wants to introduce a dramatic element into the narrative. Of the two, the *be*-form makes the speaker seem less involved. An interesting point is that the more dynamic *go* usages are often accompanied by an interjection or similar vocal effect—76 per cent of instances, in one study:

Two minutes in, he goes, 'Wow, this is strenuous' and stopped.
And he goes, 'Gosh, I've never seen you in one of those...'
And I go 'Hello, this is odd...'
And John goes [whistles]...

The use of *be*-forms also leaves open the question of whether the words were actually said out loud. This ambiguity is often present when *be*-forms are used. In the 'give me a smoke' and 'Martin Sharp' examples above, it isn't entirely clear whether the words are thought or spoken. With *say*-forms and *go*-forms, the ambiguity is resolved: the words have to be audible.

I therefore don't share the gloom of those who see quotative forms as a sign of poor speech ability. Of course, if they're overused— as with any word in the language—they can irritate. But irritation shouldn't blind us to seeing that with quotative *be* the language has developed a fresh narrative option in informal speech. It's an increase— a tiny one, but an increase nonetheless—in the expressive richness of English. And to see young people exploiting it so often shows that they haven't lost their natural story-telling skills.

Present and past participles: being and been

THE modern form of the present participle makes its appearance in Middle English. In Old English it had a different ending, seen in *beonde*, and this continued into the next millennium in a variety of spellings, such as *beand* and *beende*, with occasional regional usage recorded even as late as the nineteenth century. But once *being* arrives, in the fifteenth century, it dominates. Apart from minor spelling changes (*beyng, beying, beeinge…*) it shows very little regional variation, other than the dropping of the final *g*—usually as a sign of uneducated speech.

The social contrast is visible in many nineteenth-century novels. We see it, for example, in Charles Dickens' *The Pickwick*

Papers (1836), where Mr Weller is having a conversation with Mr Pickwick about someone Sam Weller might marry:

> 'The lady not bein' a widder,' interposed Mr. Weller in explanation.
> 'The lady not being a widow,' said Mr. Pickwick, smiling.

In fact, the dropped *g* hasn't always been restricted to the speech of lower-class characters; it was also a fashion among upper-class speakers in the decades around the turn of the twentieth century. Here's Lord Spratte in W. Somerset Maugham's *The Bishop's Apron* (1906):

> It shows what a charmin' character I have to stand bein' ragged by my younger brother.

The aristocratic usage is often recalled by the phrase *huntin', shootin', and fishin'*.

The past participle, *been*, has had a more varied career. In its earliest forms, in Old and Middle English, it was usually preceded by a particle marking its past-time status, variously spelled *ge*, *y*, or *i*: *gebeeon*, *ybeo*, *ibien*. This gradually ceased to be used, and never appears in standard English after the fifteenth century, though echoes of it are found in later regional dialect forms, such as *abean* (in Lincolnshire), *abin* (in south-west England), and *a ben* (New England). 'What have 'ee a-bin up to?' asks John Sanboy in Walter Raymond's tales of Somerset, *Love and Quiet Life* (1894). The final *-n* also drops in many dialects, so that the form sometimes looks like *be*, as in this example from Chaucer's

Canterbury Tales, describing the Knight: 'At many a noble armee hadde he be'. And when it's used in an unstressed position, it's often spelled *bin* or *byn*: 'Having bin so rocked and shaken at sea', writes James Howell in 1645.

An unusual form of the past participle, recorded on both sides of the Atlantic, is *beed. Jim an' Nell* is (as it says on the title page) 'a dramatic poem written in the dialect of North Devon by a Devonshire man' in 1867 (in fact, William Rock). At one point an old man says 'I've beed a quarter be tha watch' ('stayed a quarter of an hour by your watch'). 'I'm sorry to hear you've beed feeling so tired', writes a contributor to a US blog forum in 2014. It became common in African-American usage. There may even be a semantic contrast between *been* and *beed* in some dialects. American poet Carolyn M. Rogers in *Negro Digest* (1969) writes: 'Black Poetry is becoming what it has always been but has not quite beed'. She seems to be trying to capture the notion of something happening—yet not completely happening—in the past. Perhaps we should call it an 'unperfected' tense form.

"PARTS OF SPEECH."

"GOOD MORNING ROSIE. SHALL I FIND YOUR MOTHER AT HOME, OR IS SHE GONE
OUT?"

"NO, 'M, SHE DIDN'T BEEN. I SAW SHE AT THE WINDOW WHEN I WAS A WENTIN'."

Being

We are too late for the gods, and too
early for Being. Being's poem,
just begun, is man.

Martin Heidegger (1899–1976)
Poetry, Language, Thought (1971)

> Good humour ... is the *balm of being*, the quality
> to which all that adorns or elevates mankind
> must owe its power of pleasing.
>
> Samuel Johnson (1709–84)
> *The Rambler*, 72, 24 November 1750, paragraph 2

The whirr of flapping leathern bands and hum of
dynamos from the powerhouse urged Stephen to
be on. Beingless beings.

James Joyce (1882–1941)
Ulysses (1922), episode 10

> The translator imports new and alternative
> options of being.
>
> George Steiner (1929–)
> *After Babel* (1975), Chapter 3

The Unbearable Lightness of Being
Novel title (1984): Milan Kundera (1929–)

> *Being and Nothingness* [*L'être et le néant*]
> Title of a philosophical work (1943): Jean-Paul Sartre
> (1905–80)

Being is the great explainer.

Henry David Thoreau (1817–62)
Journal entry, 26 February 1841

Been

For of all sad words of tongue or pen,
The saddest are these: 'It might have been!'

John Greenleaf Whittier (1807–92)
'Maud Muller' (1856), l.105

> She was obviously a 'been-to', probably trained
> in England.
>
> Margaret Laurence (1926–87)
> *This Side Jordan* (1960), Chapter 14

For what has been—thanks!
For what shall be—yes!

Dag Hammarskjöld (1905–61)
Vägmarken (1950), translated as *Markings* (1964)

> The day becomes more solemn and serene
> When noon is past—there is a harmony
> In autumn, and a lustre in its sky,
> Which through the summer is not heard or seen,
> As if it could not be, as if it had not been!
>
> Percy Bysshe Shelley (1792–1822)
> 'Hymn to Intellectual Beauty' (1816)

Fuimus
We have been
The motto of several aristocratic houses

20

Woe is me
befalling *be*

Today, *me* is the only pronoun on whom woe regularly falls; but in earlier times, it could befall anyone—or anything. *Me* is 1st person singular, and instances of *woe is me* have been recorded since the early Middle Ages. Ophelia is one of the best-known users, in Shakespeare's *Hamlet* (*c.*1600), when she reflects on the prince's apparent madness:

O, woe is me,
T' have seen what I have seen, see what I see!

But we also find 1st person plural:

Woe were vs, if wee were at the rule and gouernement of creatures…
(pamphleteer Philip Stubbes, in *The Anatomie of Abuses*, 1583)

2nd person singular, both *thou* and *you*:

'Wo thee be'   (In John Gower's *Confessio Amantis* (1390), an old woman curses the knight Florent for discovering a secret)

...woe be to your Prick-ears, Sirrah!   (John Crowne, in his comedy *Sir Courtly Nice* (1685), has the zealot Hothead so threaten the fanatick Testimony)

3rd person, both singular and plural:

Woe is him whose bed is made in hell.   (Sir Henry Montagu, in his memoir on death and immortality, *Manchester Al Mundo*, 1636)

...woe be them that make the good Creatures of God instrumentes of damnation to themselues, by not vsing them but abusing them.   (Philip Stubbes again)

The construction is very old, its strange syntax being a memory of the Old English dative case, expressing the notion of 'to' or 'for'. 'Wa bið þæm' says the *Beowulf* storyteller—'woe be to them' who put their soul in danger of hellfire. He immediately follows it up with 'Wel bið þæm'—'well be to them' who seek the Lord. The collocation echoes down the centuries, especially in Bible translations:

O well is the [thee], happie art thou.   (Coverdale, 1535, Psalms 127.2)
Well is him that hath found prudence.   (King James, 1611, Ecclesiasticus 25.9)

With the disappearance of the dative in Middle English, a preposition takes its place, usually *to*, sometimes *unto*. The King James Bible has both:

Woe be unto thee, O Moab.   (Jeremiah, 48.46)
Woe be to the shepherds of Israel that do feed themselves.   (Ezekiel, 34.2)

Even physical objects could be the target of the woe. In his *Poetical Works* (1785), David Garrick reports an altercation between an actor (Heartly), who evidently keeps the back-hair of his wig in a small bag, and a critic (Wormwood), who wears his wig with the back-hair gathered together and tied in a knot with a ribbon:

> Heartly: I dislike tye-wigs; but should I throw your's into the fire, because
> I chuse to wear a bag?
> Wormwood: Woe be to your bag, if you did.

Today, *woe is me* is the standard archaic form, though *woe be me* hasn't entirely disappeared—there's even a mention of it in the online Urban Dictionary—and *woe is you* can be heard as part of a tease. For most people, such expressions are self-consciously jocular laments. But they can turn up in some unexpected places, such as this headline in the *Fiscal Times* in 2010:

> Woe is Them on $250,000 a Year

Nor would I have expected them to appear in popular music; but a track by the American rock band The Strange Boys in 2009 is titled 'Woe is You and Me', and Canadian singer Leslie Feist has a song in her album *Metals* in 2011 called simply 'Woe Be'—the salient line being 'Woe be to the girl who loves a songwriter'.

Several other words introduce the befalling sense of *be*, such as *praise*, *grace*, and *glory*. Commonly used liturgical expressions include 'Glory be to…' and 'Peace be to you' or '…with you'. Indeed, the earliest instance recorded in the *OED* is of this kind, in the Old English poem *The Phoenix*: 'Sib si þe, soð god'—'Peace be to you, true God'. A shortened form, used as an exclamation, is first recorded in the late nineteenth century: 'Glory be!'

An interesting medieval usage that seems to have completely disappeared is to have befalling *be* in a question, with *what* as the subject, to suggest a negative outcome—a misfortune. In one of the texts of the medieval poem *Cursor Mundi* (*c*.1325) a lady cries out so loudly that people ask her 'What is ȝou?'—'What's the matter with you?' And indeed a different manuscript of the poem reads 'Quat ayles ȝou?'—'What ails you?' 'Whassup?' some would say, these days. A few years later, Chaucer, in the opening paragraphs of *The Book of the Duchess*, asks himself why he can't sleep at nights:

Men might aske me why so I may not slepe and what me is.

The last three words could be glossed as 'what's wrong with me?'

That might be the end of the story of befalling *be*, if it were not for pedantic interference. In the eighteenth century, prescriptive grammarians, describing English as if it were Latin, began to insist on having *be* followed by the nominative case: *it is I* instead of the more natural and ancient *it is me*. Anyone with a philological awareness of the history of English would of course know that *woe is me* didn't have the same syntactic origin as *it is me*; but pedants who lacked this knowledge couldn't see the difference. So they said *woe is me* was wrong; it should be *woe is I*. They still do. A contributor to the Urban Dictionary—calling himself (sic) Urstupid—points out that 'the grammar is incorrect' because 'really, it's *woe is I*'. And a best-selling book on usage, by Patricia T. O'Connor (1996, now in its third edition), is actually called *Woe Is I*.

What is *woe is me*, with all its literary and biblical overtones, doing in an online avant-garde dictionary renowned for its scatological content? Because there is a present-day phenomenon glossed as 'The act of feeling sorry for yourself for no particular reason, save for the fact you have nothing to keep your mind off your past'. It is solemnly listed as *woe-is-me'ing*.

21

All shall be well
membership *be*

Logicians draw attention to the big difference between sentences like *I am David Crystal* (Chapter 4) and *I am a man*. The second one allows expansion into 'I am a member of the class of entities called *man*'. The first doesn't. There is no class of entities called *David Crystal*, as far as I'm aware. *Be* in the first case has an equative or identifying function. In the second case it allows us to convey the idea of membership. But membership of what?

Noun classes, most obviously, reinforced by the indefinite article. 'What do you want to be when you grow up?' we ask a child. 'I want to be a linguist': that is, 'I want to be a member of the class of linguists'. This is an ancient usage, found throughout Old English, and recurring in homilies and Bible translations: 'I am a poor man', 'you are a stranger', 'he is a prophet'... And throughout the history of English, *OED* citations show it in a great variety of contexts: 'Syracuse was a noble city', 'Intemperance is a great vice', 'I have been an undeserving rebel'...

A late development of this usage places a really strong stress on the verb. The first recorded instance is this one, from *Life of the Rev. George Crabbe* (1834):

> Before he retired at night, he had generally the pleasure of half an hour's confidential conversation with Sir Walter, when he spoke occasionally of the Waverly novels … These *were* evenings.

And a present-day citation shows how the usage has survived, from an automobile magazine:

> Big motor up front, six gears in your mit … this *is* a sportscar.   (*Driven*, 2006)

The meaning is that the noun phrase following the verb is to be taken as a superior or remarkable example of its class. It's special.

This stressed use of *be* is very different from the emphasis we can give the verb when we're making a semantic contrast such as a contradiction:

> Speaker A: That isn't a sportscar.
> Speaker B: It *is* a sportscar.

When someone admiringly says 'You *are* a good worker', it is a spontaneous utterance. Nobody has just denied it.

Adjectives too permit the notion of membership. If I say 'The car is new' I am in effect saying that the car is a member of the class of entities that can be called 'new'. It's another ancient usage, illustrated by an example from the West Saxon Gospels (Matthew 11):

> Soþlice min geoc ys wynsum, & min byrþyn ys leoht.
> 'Truly my yoke is easy and my burden is light.'

Examples are just as various as with the nouns: 'I'm curious', 'Are you deaf?', 'She'll be ready', 'They weren't very comfortable', 'All shall be well'.

"You on guard to-night, Nobby?"   "Naw."
"Wot yer bin an' washed yer face for, then?"

The present and past subjunctive: be it noted, if I were you…

THE subjunctive mood is a way of talking about events that are not matters of fact, such as wishes, conditions, and hypothetical states—in English, often introduced by a conditional word such as *if*. It was a notable grammatical feature of Old English, as it was expressed through its own distinctive forms. If people said *ic eom*, they would mean 'I am'; if they said *ic sy* or *ic beo* it would mean more 'I might be' or 'I could be'. Similarly *we sindon* 'we are' contrasted with *we syn* or *we beon*. And in the past tense *ic wæs* 'I was' contrasted with *ic wære* 'I were' and *we wæron* with *we wæren*. We see two subjunctives in this sentence:

him wære bettere þæt he næfre geboren wære
Literally: for-him were better that he never born were
'It would have been better for him if he had never been born.'

During the Old English period, the functions of the subjunctive were gradually taken over by auxiliary verbs, such as *might* and *could*, and in later periods these became the usual way of expressing non-factual meanings. Only remnants of the subjunctive remain in Modern English, in such expressions as 'Heaven help us' (vs 'Heaven helps us'), and most notably, in the continued use of forms of *be*, as in the King James Bible (1 Samuel 23): 'Blessed be yee of the Lord'. We still have that usage today, in both present and past tenses:

The heavens be praised! (*vs* The heavens are praised.)
If that be the official view… (*vs* That is the official view.)
If she were living in London… (*vs* She was living in London.)

Be-forms provide the main evidence for the presence of the subjunctive in Modern English.

Regional dialects have been especially conservative in the use of the subjunctive, and display it in a wide variety of forms. For example, we find *bees*, *beez*, and *biz* all recorded in Ulster Scots in such contexts as 'if it be', and *bisna*, *bissent*, and *bisn't* for the negative ('if it be not'). With the negative particle attached we find such forms as *beean't* and *binnot* in Yorkshire, *binna* in Northumberland, *binnae* in Scotland, and *baint* and *beant* in Ireland. 'Cat my dogs, if I baint ding-bushed like everything!' writes James Joyce in *Finnegans Wake* (1939).

In the past tense, similarly, we find considerable regional variation, with *were* appearing also in such forms as *war* and *wor* in northern England, and *wair* and *weir* in Scotland. The pronoun *it* is often attached, to produce *twere* or *'twere*, and regional *twar* and *'twar*. Lines from Shakespeare's *Macbeth* come to mind, showing how the demands of the metre foster the reduced form:

If it were done when 'tis done, then 'twere well
It were done quickly.

It is also found attached after the verb, resulting in *wert* or *were't*, again with regional variations such as *wart*. It's a usage that today is unlikely to be found outside of poetry or the occasional representation of olden speech.

The use of a preceding negative particle attached to the past tense form (as in *nære* or *nere*) died out in Middle English. Forms such as *wan't* and *wern't* begin to appear in the sixteenth century, and *weren't* is soon established as the norm, with some regional variation, mainly reflecting local pronunciations (as in *warn't*, *worn't*, and *wurnt*) but sometimes echoing older forms (as in *warna* and *wurden*).

What is immediately apparent, though, is that the past tense forms no longer make any distinction in standard English between indicative (see Panels on p. 92 and on p. 110) and subjunctive in the 2nd person singular and in the plural: the same form appears in both *you were going* and *if you were going*, so unless the rest of the sentence makes it absolutely clear, we can't say for sure which mood is intended. This isn't a problem with the 1st and 3rd persons singular, where standard English clearly contrasts *was* and *were*.

I was/wasn't going. *vs* I wish I were/weren't going.

And similarly, in the present tense, we see other possible contrasts:

I am going tomorrow. *vs* I wish I were going tomorrow.
He is ready. *vs* I insist that he be ready.

As with the past indicative (Panels on p. 92 and on p. 110), the past subjunctive allows a stylistic contrast between *was* and *were*, with *were* being the more formal option:

I wish I were/weren't going. vs *I wish I was/wasn't going.*

A unique feature of the subjunctive is that it promotes inverted word order. Instead of saying 'Whether they are alive or dead…' we can say 'Be they alive or dead…'. Instead of 'If you were to leave now…' we can say 'Were you to leave now…'. Again, the usage is rather formal or literary, but through song and proverbial repetition some instances have become widely familiar: 'Be it ever so humble, there's no place like home.' And for a century or more, English-speaking children have loved this scary verse from the fairy tale 'Jack and the Beanstalk':

Fee-Fi-Fo-Fum,
I smell the blood of an Englishman.
Be he alive or be he dead,
I'll grind his bones to make my bread.

22

How old are you?
chronological *be*

When a form of *be* is used with a phrase specifying a period of time in numbers (years, months, days, centuries...), its meaning narrows significantly. Now the expression conveys the amount of time someone or something has existed—the age the entity has attained. 'How old is he?'—'He's thirty-two.'

People are the obvious candidates, and have been since Old English. The *Anglo-Saxon Chronicle* for the year 972 (the Laud text, my translation) tells us how

> Edgar the atheling was consecrated king at Bath, on Pentecost's mass-day, on the 5th before the Ides of May, the thirteenth year since he had obtained the kingdom; and he was then one less thirty winters. [& he wæs þa ana wana xxx wintra]

In Chaucer's 'The Monk's Tale', we're told that the imprisoned Earl of Pisa had three children, 'The eldest scarsly fyf yeer was of age'. In Shakespeare's *The Taming of the Shrew*, Vincentio says he has brought his servant Tranio up 'ever since he was three years old'.

Gradually the usage extended to places and things, such as ancient monuments. The present tense comes to be used alongside the past. Stonehenge, for example, would be said to 'be' so many thousand years old. Draw the ale from a barrel, says a 1653 source, 'when the Ale is two dayes old'. Animals are described in the same way: lion cubs 'scarcely begin to walk till they are two months old', reports a writer in 1795.

The omission of the noun of time is recorded from the seventeenth century. Stephen Penton, in *The Guardian's Instruction or The Gentleman's Romance* (1688, 'written for the diversion and service of the gentry'), recommends how a young man should behave when he goes to Oxford University, drawing especial attention to the dangers that can befall him if he fails to look after his horse properly:

> This was the unhappiness of a delicate Youth, whose great misfortune it was to be worth Two Thousand A Year before he was *One and Twenty*.

That's the norm today. If someone says 'She's fifteen', we assume it means years. Anything else needs to be specified: 'How old's your baby?'—'Nine months'. Even though it's obviously a baby, nobody would ever say 'nine'.

The usage also appears in relation to future time: 'She'll be eleven next month'. But a quirk of English grammar makes this form unnecessary when the futurity is implied in a time conjunction such as *until* or *before*. 'You'll be staying at that school until you're fifteen', 'You'll not leave before you're fifteen'. A common error in those learning English as a foreign language is to say: '. . . until you will be fifteen', '. . . before you will be fifteen'. Similarly, learners need to note the quirk with past time: 'I've lived in this town since I was five'. Despite the fact that the sentence begins with a *have* form, we don't say 'I've lived in this town since I've been five'. Evidently, we think of a past age as something distantly removed from the present, and not a time that still has current relevance to us.

There's also an interesting construction that allows us to talk about an entity in terms of an unspecified future time—a kind of future equivalent of 'as was' (Chapter 2):

I'd like you to meet my bride-to-be.
I'm her father-to-be.

Shakespeare is the first recorded user, in Sonnet 81:

And tongues to be your being shall rehearse

The *to-be* part is an unusual adjectival use, shown by the way it can occur before the noun as well: examples from the nineteenth century include 'the to be Mrs Berry' (that one from Lord Nelson) and 'the four to-be priests'. There's a nice example of the time contrast in dramatist Lillian Hellman's memoir *An Unfinished Woman* (1969):

The so-called good life for us is the to-be-good life for them.

As the Shakespeare example illustrates, not only people can be 'to-be'. I once heard someone, looking dolefully at a mound of canvas and pegs in a campsite, in the rain, and wondering where to start, say 'This is our tent-to-be'.

The general sense is one of 'coming into existence in due course'— or its opposite, of course, *not* coming into existence. *Be as be may*, as the old sixteenth-century saying goes. Both positive and negative forms are common:

...your husband that shall be. (Mrs Malaprop describes Captain Absolute in Richard Brinsley Sheridan's *The Rivals*, 1775)

The quiet, the retirement of such a life would have answered all my ideas
of happiness! But it was not to be.   (Wickham reflects on living in
Kympton in Jane Austen's *Pride and Prejudice*, 1813)

Chronological *be* raises an issue that doesn't often arise when dis-
cussing the functions of this verb: appropriateness. The question is
not only 'What does this use of the verb mean?' but 'When is it proper
to use the verb in this way?' There are certain restrictions. In particular, we can't actually go around asking people their age.

Children learn this lesson very early in life. At a birthday party,
grown-ups persist in asking the new four-year-old how old he or she
is. 'I'm four' is the expected reply. But if the child were to ask cooing
granny how old *she* is, the answer will be along the lines of 'Oh no,
dear, you mustn't ask ladies their age'. It's interesting that, whenever
someone asks for an age, the context is typically one where there is an
element of suspicion or danger:

A young-looking man asks a shopkeeper for a bottle of wine. 'How old are
you?' asks the shopkeeper, sceptically.

A group of teenagers try to get into a club where everyone has to be at
least eighteen. 'How old are you?' asks the doorman, belligerently.

A doctor looks at the weight-to-height results of a patient, and asks
'How old are you, Mr Crystal?', in a tired, how-many-times-do-I-have-
to-tell-you-to-do-more-exercise tone of voice.

In linguistics, such factors would be analysed under the heading of
pragmatics, the study of the choices we make when we use language.
On the whole, the use of *be* raises few pragmatic issues; but they are
important here.

[HELENA]
    You are my mother, madam; would you were—
    So that my lord your son were not my brother—
    Indeed my mother! Or were you both our mothers
    I care no more for than I do for heaven,
    So I were not his sister.

William Shakespeare (1564–1616)
All's Well that Ends Well, 1.3.156

                    If you were the only girl in the world
                    and I were the only boy
                    Nothing else would matter in the world today
                    We could go on loving in the same old way

                    Nat D. Ayer (1887–1952) and Clifford Grey (1887–1941)
                    The Bing Boys Are Here (1916)

O thus be it ever, when freemen shall stand
Between their loved homes and the war's
desolation.
Blest with vict'ry and peace, may the Heav'n
rescued land
Praise the Power that hath made and preserved
us a nation!

Francis Scott Key (1779–1843)
'The Star-spangled Banner' (1814)

23

Is you is or is you ain't?
musical *be*

What is it about auxiliary verbs that attracts the lyricist? It's easy to see the point with content verbs, such as *love*, which provide the theme of thousands of songs. But grammatical words?

In the days of music hall in Britain, auxiliary verbs were an important part of the song-writer's tool-kit, probably because they could be used elliptically, without the associated main verb, and thus allow all kinds of double entendres. Here's the chorus to one popular song, composed in 1907 by George Arthurs and performed by Lily Lena. The opening lines provide the theme:

> She was a maid who was very, very staid
> So different to the youth beside her…

The chorus runs:

> 'I don't think I would, and I'm not sure that I should
> For it isn't quite just the thing that's right
> So I would not if I could, could, could

If you think it's fun, I don't
And my answer is I won't
For I know I can't
And I'm sure I shan't'
And the finish was, she did!

There are just two verses in the official version: in the first, he asks to hold her hand; in the second, he offers her a glass of wine. As with many music-hall songs, unofficial versions went further.

But a desire for risqué cheekiness can't account for all the songs that focus on a form of *be*. The short forms seem to have a phonetic appeal of their own, especially when used repeatedly. Here's a verse from 'And it Was', performed by Jay Laurier in 1919:

I'm brim full of talent, I'd soon be the rage
Once at a Music Hall I got to learn
That they could find room for just one extra turn
I went round on Saturday night
And the Manager said, 'It's all right
I think that it's time now for your turn to sing.'
And it was, and it was
He said, 'Sing a love song from 'twill be just the thing'
And it was, and it was
I can't remember all that occurred
A cabbage hit me and a strange noise I heard
And a young fellow said, 'Why that must be the "bird"'
And it was, and it was.

There are two more verses like that.

The present tense gets the same treatment. Here's the chorus of 'We are, we are, we are' (1881), also known as 'The Merry Family', performed by Arthur Roberts:

Fanny plays the honey-pots, Loo's the gal to skip
Bob's the finest whistler that ever cocked a lip
Jane can play a tune or two upon the gay guitar
Oh, we are such a merry family, we are, we are, we are.

Puns were highly valued, especially if there was an unusual word or name that chimed with the verb, as in Arthur Le Clerq's 1929 hit 'Is Izzy Azzy Wozz?', recorded by The Ever-Bright Boys, which begins:

Is Mr Izzy ill, is he, is he?
Has he caught a chill, has he, has he?

After some medical suggestions, the drama continues:

Is he breathing still, is he? is he?
Will he make a will, will he? will he?

The song's title is eventually explained:

I am Izzy's lawyer and I've called around because
I want to know is Izzy worse or is he as he was?

A different Izzy is the hero of a 1924 hit performed by Carl Fenton's orchestra with vocal chorus, which begins:

Whose Izzy is he (is he yours or is he mine?)
I'm getting dizzy watching Izzy all the time

People knew it as 'Whose Izzy is he?'.

The attraction can be seen in later songs, such as 'Is you is or is you ain't my baby?' (1944) by Louis Jordan and Billy Austin, with the original dialect background clear in the chorus (later versions often substituted standard English):

Is you is or is you ain't my baby?
The way you're actin' lately makes me doubt

You's is still my baby, baby
Seems my flame in your heart's done gone out.

British radio comedian Arthur Askey (1938) had a hit with his 'Bee Song' in 1938:

Oh, what a wonderful thing to be,
A healthy grown up busy busy bee;
Whiling away all the passing hours
Pinching all the pollen from the cauliflowers.
I'd like to be a busy little bee,
Being as busy as a bee can be.

But the high point of musical *be*-exploitation was definitely the period in the decades around 1900. Idiomatic phrases were especially popular. Here's one verse and chorus of E. W. Rogers' 'As You Were Before', performed by Arthur Tinsley in the 1890s:

When out at night with dear old pals you get a drop too much
You tell them you're quite sober, and with help you walk as such
And propped against your door you stand, as straight as any die
But if that door be opened, in the twinkling of an eye

(*Spoken*) You must be—

Chorus: As you were before, as you were before
Something seems uneven as you walk upon the floor
And the wife says, 'Mr T., I can very plainly see
That you are—as you've been before.'

And here's a verse from 'I Wish I Was', performed by George Leybourne in the 1870s, which rings the changes on *am* and *be*:

I'm not satisfied at all with what I am, but could
I only be what I am not depend on it, I would

For madly I'm in love, as deep as deep can be
But sure enough I find to my cost the girl don't care for me.

The chorus explains the title:

I wish I was a bee, from her lips to gather honey,
Or like the great Baron Rothschild, with heaps of ready money;
I wish I was a train, or a bath chair I would be,
I wish I was a hansom cab, that she should ride in me.

Nobody exploited auxiliary verbs more than W. S. Gilbert in Act 2 of the comic opera *Princess Ida* (1884). The Princess asks 'Who lectures in the Hall of Arts to-day?' and Lady Blanche replies:

I, madam, on Abstract Philosophy.
There I propose considering, at length,
Three points—The Is, the Might Be, and the Must.
Whether the Is, from being actual fact,
Is more important than the vague Might Be,
Or the Might Be, from taking wider scope,
Is for that reason greater than the Is:
And lastly, how the Is and Might Be stand
Compared with the inevitable Must!

And this prompts a song:

Come mighty Must! Inevitable Shall!
In thee I trust.
Time weaves my coronal!
Go, mocking Is!
Go, disappointing Was!
That I am this
Ye are the cursèd cause!

Yet humble second shall be first, I wean
And dead and buried be the curst Has Been!
Oh, weak Might Be!
Oh, May, Might, Could, Would, Should!
How powerless ye
For evil or for good!
In every sense
Your moods I cheerless call,
Whate'er your tense
Ye are Imperfect all!
Ye have deceived the trust I've shown in ye!
Away! The Mighty Must alone Shall be!

Nothing has yet beaten that.

24
Oh no he isn't
ludic *be*

Forms of *be* have been a fruitful source of playful language, more than with any other verb. The phonetic coincidence of *be* and *are* with the names of two letters of the alphabet has for centuries been exploited in rebus puzzles (visual puns), which often included the use of single letters to stand for syllables or words. These were especially popular in Victorian England, and continued into the twentieth century in innumerable annuals and puzzle books, presenting such conundrums as:

YYURYYUBICURYY4 me ('Too wise you are...')

In the twenty-first century, rebuses have gained a new lease of life with text messaging and other Internet interactions where it's fashionable and time-saving to use abbreviations.

The phonetic identity of *be* with *bee* has been another source of playfulness. Probably every conceivable pun has by now been explored, and the juxtaposition of the two words has fuelled generations of jokers:

What do you call a bee that can't make up its mind?
A maybe!

Knock, knock.
Who's there?
Honey bee.
Honey bee who?
Honey, be a dear and get me a drink.

I didn't say they were funny.

One of these jokes illustrates a further kind of playfulness: the adaptation of a famous quotation:

What did the confused bee say to its mate?
To bee or not to bee.

There have been many variants. My favourite is Homer Simpson's self-directed question as he arrives at a bar: 'Two beers or not two beers?' But any well-known quotation using a distinctive form of *be* can expect to receive the same treatment, as in the opening line of Shelley's ode to the skylark (Panel on p. 110): 'Hail to thee, blithe spirit! Bird thou never wert'. American poet Rennie McQuilkin writes in 'Good Friday' (2013), after hearing the sound of a bird at night:

If such sounds come to me in my problematic state
and no one else to hear, does this bird-thou-never-wertness
exist at all? Or I?

And Ogden Nash imagines the lark celebrated by Oscar Hammerstein II in *The Sound of Music* having a verbal duel with the lark addressed by Shelley (in 'Hark, hark, the larks do bark', 1968):

Its very salutation was pert:

'Hail to thee, whatever thou mayest be, because it's on record that bird
thou never wert.
Thou wert never even a gnatcatcher or a goatsucker or a godwit or yet
a skua bird.'
And the Shelley lark said, 'I am too a bird!'
And the Hammerstein lark said, 'I will argue to and fro not.
Shelley himself admits that what thou art we know not.'

Other forms of *be* can lead to puns. The phonetic identity between
Izzy and *is he*, a feature of some music-hall songs (Chapter 23), turns
up quite often, as *Izzy* is a short form of many first names, such as
Isaac, Israel, Isabel, Isidore, and *Elizabeth*. So we often see such online
wisecracks as 'Izzy real', 'Izzy busy', and 'Who Izzy?'. Episode 23 (2004)
of the Rugrats spin-off *All Grown Up!*, a children's animated TV series
for Nickelodeon, was called 'Izzy or Isn't He?'. The title reflects the
storyline that Dil's imaginary alien friend, Izzy, has had a fatal acci-
dent—or (being imaginary) has he? And the name even turns up in
English language teaching, as part of present-tense exercises:

Captain Izzy is, he is, he is
Captain Izzy is, he is, he is
He is a Grammar Master, the super-hero kind.
And he is, he is, he is
He is a friend of mine.

Was gets in on the act, thanks to the fortuitous phonetic identity
between *was he* ('wuz he') and *wuzzy*, most famously in the eighteenth-
century nursery rhyme:

Fuzzy Wuzzy was a bear,
Fuzzy Wuzzy had no hair,
Fuzzy Wuzzy wasn't fuzzy, wuz he?

It's no longer just bears: virtually anything can be introduced in this way. In various online contexts, fuzzy wuzzy wuz—a kitten, a bunny, a sheep, a sweater...A 2008 headline ran: 'Fuzzy Wuzzy Wuz a Kindle 2', referring to the supposed fuzziness of certain fonts. A pet-grooming service in Missouri is called 'Fuzzy Wuz He'. In Wisconsin, an annual winter open horse show for extra-furry animals is called 'How Fuzzy Wuz He'.

The other form of *be* that attracts puns is *been*, thanks to the phonetic identity with *bean*. Most joke-books contain this one:

Customer: Waiter, what do you call this soup?
Waiter: It's bean soup, sir.
Customer: I don't care what it's been. What is it now?

And there is no shortage of variants along the lines of:

What did one bean say to another bean he hadn't seen for a long time?
How you been?
What did the father bean say to the teenage bean who came in after
    midnight?
Where you been?

The other forms of *be* aren't usually candidates for punning, but they do have a role in some ludic genres. Limericks often rely on *was*: 'There was—a young lady from Reading, an old soldier from Ipswich...'. Traditional word-building riddles rely on *is* and *am*:

My first is in blue but not in glue;
My second is in old but not in new;
My third is in look but not in see;
My last is in ask but not in plea;
My whole has leaves but not a flower;

'Twill help you pass an idle hour.
What am I?

Children seem to sense the power of contrasting forms of *be* at an early age, as in this exchange between two four-year-olds:

That's my apple.
Tisn't
Tis
Tisn't
Tis...

It's an interaction that feeds directly into the British pantomime tradition, where the audience doesn't need to be told how to react when someone or something scary appears behind one of the 'good' characters, who denies it is there: they already know.

Audience: He's behind you!
Good character: Oh no he isn't!
Audience: Oh yes he is!
Good character: OH NO HE ISN'T!
Audience: OH YES HE IS!

A hysterical use of *be*.

She. "I wish you'd tell me what you think of Mrs. Spiffington."
He. "Well, she looks—what? But of course she really isn't."
She. "Oh, but that's just what she is."

25

Lane closed ahead
missing *be*

There's a story attributed to the American journalist Robert Benchley, who arrived in Venice for the first time and sent a telegram to his editor at the *New Yorker*: 'Streets full of water. Please advise.' The story has been associated with others, but whoever the original source was, the relevant linguistic point in the telegram remains the same: the *are* is omitted.

In the days when senders were charged by the word, it paid them to be as elliptical as possible. Grammatical words such as *the*, *a*, and the various forms of *be* were omitted whenever it didn't cause ambiguity. Of course, if money wasn't an issue, you kept them in. But the typical style was to omit, giving rise to the labels 'telegramese' and 'telegraphese'.

Today, textese has replaced telegramese. The pressure is no longer financial, but ergonomic and technological: it saves time and energy to dispense with words that aren't critical to the sense, and the software imposes a limit on the length of a message—160 characters for texts, 140 for tweets. 'On train' is much easier to type than 'I am on the train'. And in a longer message, where we might be struggling to complete our thought within the character limit, the saving offered by omitting *be*-forms is attractive indeed.

A different kind of spatial constraint occurs with notices such as road signs. We're unlikely to see 'Lane is closed ahead' or 'Queues are likely'. Apart from the need to fit the message into the space allowed by the sign (whether physical or electronic), there's a psycholinguistic motivation: focusing on the important words allows quicker assimilation of the message, especially when travelling at 70 miles an hour.

Newspaper headlines and advertising posters motivate the same minimalism. We will see '20 killed' or 'Minister sacked'. Or something like this:

'XMAS ALL ABOUT SALES' SAYS BISHOP

No he didn't. He would have said 'Xmas is ...'. Or maybe 'has been' or 'will be'? That's another benefit of the elliptical construction: it avoids the writer having to choose between tenses.

We can handle 'missing *be*' without a second thought because it has been part of our linguistic upbringing from the earliest days. Indeed, the early sentences of children have been called 'telegraphic' by scholars studying child language acquisition. Some typical sentences from a two-year-old: 'Man running', 'Car broken', 'Dolly foot sore', 'Red car in garage'.

Then, when language has been acquired, we routinely leave out a *be*-form with its subject in colloquial speech at the beginning of a sentence. We can omit an *I am* ('Sorry I can't be with you'), an *are you* ('Pleased to see me?'), or an *it is* ('Good to see you'). *Is there* disappears when we say 'Anyone in?' The subject stays without its verb in 'You going out?', 'That you, Fred?', and 'Where we going?'. The imperative form is dropped in 'Careful!'. A tiny remnant of the verb is heard when we say such things as "S alright". We can even leave out the verb in more formal and longer sentences:

Although tired, I went out. = Although I was tired, I went out.

It's one of the ways of achieving a more succinct style.

Some varieties of English routinely omit *be*-forms. We will hear sentences like these in many pidgin and creole languages derived from English:

I no fine. [= I'm not well]
She waitin for me right now.
This a number one good book.

In this respect, English is beginning to resemble languages that make no use of a copula in the present tense, such as Russian, where a sentence such as *I am a doctor* would be (in an English transliteration) *ya doktor*.

There's a famous pastiche of pidgin English in the meeting of two characters in a story by Edgar Rice Burroughs: 'Me Tarzan, you Jane'. These words aren't actually used in his novels, but they have achieved widespread currency through cinema. It seems obligatory for any non-standard-English-speaking character, such as the 'bad guys' in spaghetti westerns, to speak with *be*-forms omitted. Aliens are no exception. If we meet the inhabitants of a distant galaxy, in a sci-fi movie, their English is usually not very good, so we may well hear them say such things as 'You from planet Earth'. Well, some aliens. Yoda from *Star Wars* likes to keep his *be*'s, but puts them at the end: 'Full of the force, you are'.

26

It's just a book, is all
summarizing *be*

During the twentieth century, a new idiomatic use of *be* emerged in colloquial North American English—an elliptical form of 'that is all' or (less commonly) 'that was all'. A handful of *OED* examples illustrate the usage, first recorded in John Fante's novel *Wait until Spring, Bandini* (1939):

> Here is a ring I bought you ... Expensive? Naaaw. Three hundred, is all.

The intention is to turn a negative situation into a positive one: the situation is not as bad as might have been thought.

It's used in quite a wide range of attitudinal contexts—dismissive, grudging, justifying, apologetic—always with a summarizing force ('that is all there is to be said'):

> One night, she threw away his letters. It wasn't a planned decision. She was just cleaning her bureau, was all, and couldn't think of any good reason to save them.   (Anne Tyler, *Dinner at the Homesick Restaurant*, 1982)

When he gets like that there's no tellin' what he'll do. We got scared is
all.   (Nevada Barr, *Deep South*, 2000)

The usage has proved to be very popular, steadily growing around the
English-speaking world. It has an appealing conciseness, and suggests an easy-going, laid-back rapport between speaker and listener.
It lacks the abruptness of *that is all* (*there is to be said*). I find myself
using it quite often, these days, though never, until now, in a book.

There's nothing more I can think of to say about it. It makes a
succinct final chapter, is all.

Squire. "WELL, MATTHEW, AND HOW ARE YOU NOW?"
Convalescent. "THANKEE, SIR, I BE BETTER THAN I WERE, BUT I BEANT AS WELL AS I
  WERE AFORE I WAS BAD AS I BE NOW."

APPENDIX

Early English pronunciations

A number of the examples in this book are from Old and Middle English texts. This appendix gives approximate word-pronunciations using the International Phonetic Alphabet.

& *see* and
ætbeon /atˈbeːən/
age /ˈɑːʒə/
allterr /ˈaltɛɹ/
an /ɑːn/
ana /ˈɑnːə/
and [&] /ɑnd/
aren /ˈarən/
arð /aɹθ/
aryn /ˈarən/
ayles /aɪlz/

be /beː/
beam /beːəm/
bee /beː/
ben /beːn/
bene /ˈbeːnə/
beo / beːə/
beom /beːəm/
beon /beːən/
beonde /ˈbeːəndə/
beonne /ˈbeːənə/

beoð /beːəθ/
beoðan /ˈbeːəðən/
bettere /ˈbɛtərə/
bian /biːən/
biað, bieð, bioð /biːəθ/
bion /biːən/
bist /bɪst/
bið /bɪθ/
biðon /ˈbɪðən/
bium /biːəm/
byrþyn /ˈbyɹθɪn/, /ˈbyɹðɪn/
byð /byθ/

com /koːm/
cumen /ˈkʊmən/

ðu /θuː/

eam /ɛːəm/
earan, earon /ˈɛːərən/
eart /ɛːəɹt/

175

earð /ɛːəɹθ/
emme /ˈɛmə/
eom /ɛːəm/
eren, eryn /ˈɛːɹən/
ese, ess /ɛs/

fæder /ˈfædəɹ/
frambeon /framˈbeːən/
fyf /fyːv/

gang /gaŋg/
gangan /ˈgaŋgən/
gange /ˈgaŋgə/
gang-ern /ˈgaŋg-ɛːɹn/
gang-feormere /ˈgaŋg-
    fɛəɹməɹə/
gang-pyt /ˈgaŋg-pyt/
gang-setl /ˈgaŋg-setl/
gang-tun /ˈgaŋg-tuːn/
gebeeon /jəˈbiːən/
geboren /jəˈbɒrən/
geoc /jeːək/
god /gɒd/
godess /ˈgoːdəs/
gong /gɒŋg/

ȝou /juː/

Hæsten /ˈhæstən/
hal /hɑːl/
hale /ˈhɑːlə/
he /heː/
heofnum /ˈhɛəvnəm/
heofunum /ˈhɛəvənəm/

herge /ˈhɛɹɣə/
him /hɪm/
his / hɪs/

ibien /jɪˈbiːən/
ic /ɪtʃ/
icham /ˈɪtʃəm/
in /ɪn/

Krist /krɪst/

lannge /ˈlaŋgə/
leoht /leːəxt/

mæg /mæj/
maistrye /ˈmaɪstriːə/
mid /mɪd/
min /miːn/

næfre /ˈnæːvrə/
næm /næm/
nære /ˈnæːrə/
næs, nass /næs/
nart /naɹt/
nartu /ˈnaɹtʊ/
neam /nɛəm/
nert /nɛɹt/
nertu /ˈnɛɹtʊ/
nes /nɛs/

on /ɒn/

quat /ʍat/

176

rodi /ˈroːdi/

schul /ʃʊl/
se /seː/
si /siː/
sib /sɪb/
sie /siːə/
sind /sɪnd/
sindan, sindon /ˈsɪndən/
sint /sɪnt/
skarsly /ˈskɑːɹslɪ/
soð /soːθ/
soþlice /ˈsoːðlɪtʃə/
swa /swɑː/
sy /syː/
syn /syːn/
synden /ˈsyːndən/

to /toː/

þa /θɑː/
þæm /θæːm/
þær /θæːɹ/
þæt, þat /θæt/
þe [= that] /θə/
þe [=thee] /θeː/
þreade /ˈθrɛədə/
þu /θuː/

uæs /wæs/
unnderr /ˈʊndəɹ/
uoere /ˈwɛːrə/
ure /ˈuːrə/
uuærun /ˈwæːrən/

wa /wɑː/
wære /ˈwæːrə/
wæren, wæron /ˈwæːrən/
wæs, wæss /wæs/
wana /ˈwɑːnə/
wass /was/
wast /wast/
we /weː/
wel /wɛl/
were /ˈwɛːrə/
wern /wɛːrn/
wes /wɛs/
wesað /ˈwɛsəθ/
wesan /ˈweːzən/
wintra /ˈwɪntrə/
wynsum /ˈwynsəm/

xxx [thirty] /ˈθriːtɪj/

ybeo /jiˈbeːə/
ycham / ˈɪtʃəm/
yeer /jiːɹ/
ys /ys/

LIST OF ILLUSTRATIONS FROM *PUNCH*

Giles. "Wot be this 'ere about t' squire?"
Jarge. " 'E be O.B.E., e be."
Giles. "Oh, be 'e?"

PUBLISHER'S ACKNOWLEDGEMENTS

We are grateful for permission to include the following copyright material in this book:

Lines p.10 from 'Ars Poetica' (*Collected Poems 1917–1982*) by Archibald MacLeish. Copyright © 1985 by The Estate of Archibald MacLeish. Used by permission of Houghton Mifflin Harcourt Publishing Company. All rights reserved.

Line of dialogue p. 11 from *The Search for Signs of Intelligent Life in the Universe* by Jane Wagner, copyright © 1986, 1990 by Jane Wagner Inc. Reprinted by permission of HarperCollins Publishers.

Brief excerpt p.23 from *A Tale for the Time Being* by Ruth Ozeki. Copyright © 2013 by Ruth Ozeki. Used by permission of Canongate Books.

Brief excerpt p.65 from *On Aggression* by Konrad Lorenz. Copyright © 1963 by Konrad Lorenz. Used by permission of Taylor and Francis Group.

Lines p.87 from 'The Screen with the Face with the Voice' (*Good Intentions*) by Ogden Nash, copyright © 1942 by Ogden Nash, renewed. Twelve-line excerpt reprinted by permission of Curtis Brown, Ltd.

Publisher's Acknowledgements

Brief excerpt p. 135 from *Poetry, Language, Thought* by Martin Heidegger. Translations and Introduction by Albert Hofstadter. Copyright © 1971 by Martin Heidegger. Reprinted by permission of HarperCollins Publishers.

The publisher and author have made every effort to trace and contact all copyright holders before publication. If notified, the publisher will be pleased to rectify any errors or omissions at the earliest opportunity.

INDEX OF NAMES

INDEX OF SUBJECTS